D0149748

Become the
COACH
You Were Meant to Be

— *The 5 Goals of Leadership*

Paul J. Meyer
New York Times Best-Selling Author

Become The Coach You Were Meant To Be

Published by
Executive Books
206 West Allen Street
Mechanicsburg, PA 17055
717-766-9499   800-233-2665
Fax: 717-766-6565
www.ExecutiveBooks.com

Copyright © 2007 by Paul J. Meyer
All rights reserved.

All rights reserved. No part of this book may be reproduced or trans-
mitted in any form or by any means, electronic or mechanical, includ-
ing photocopying, recording, or by any information storage and
retrieval system, without the written permission of the publisher,
except where permitted by law.

ISBN-13: 978-1-933715-47-6
ISBN-10: 1-933715-47-2

Printed in the United States of America

Endorsements

Whatever Paul J. Meyer teaches is tested, proven, and profitable. If it isn't, he doesn't touch it! As a coach, listen to what Paul says ... and then implement it. Digest every word, because every word has a purpose. There are no meaningless plays in this playbook!

Don Shula, football coach

I have had the incredible privilege of teaching, training, and impacting thousands upon thousands of young people over the years. The truth is Paul J. Meyer is responsible for much of that. Without question, I consider Paul J. Meyer to be one of the top 5 most influential people in America and the world!

Homer Rice, football coach

Paul J. Meyer has produced a new leadership and management creed — a methodology that is both practical and personal. What you hold in your hands is a unique new strategy for dealing with the age-old problem of leading and motivating others.

Drayton McClane, past Vice Chairman of Wal-Mart

Paul J. Meyer has been my cornerstone of mentorship, helping me to become more and achieve more. Leadership is everything and we can all grow into leaders if we have Mr. Meyer's leadership to follow and copy. To me, Mr. Meyer is the "leader of all leaders." It's one thing learning yourself, but he teaches you how to CREATE leaders to exponentially impact your chosen endeavor. Thank you, Paul, for your undying giving attitude.

Brian Carruthers, businessman

This book is mandatory reading for anyone who is in a position of leadership, regardless of the level of responsibility.

Kenneth H. Cooper, M.D., founder of The Cooper Clinic

Here's a book that will enable you to become an empowered and empowering leader. Paul J. Meyer's powerful and proven techniques will guide you to tap and harness your God-given potential for effective leadership. By internalizing and practicing these strategies, you will achieve extraordinary success in every facet of your life and business.

Fr. Anthony A. D'Souza, management director

Paul J. Meyer's principles transcend time and cultures. Since founding my company nearly 50 years ago, I have enjoyed well-earned success. I am greatly indebted to Mr. Meyer for my business growth. I highly recommend all of Mr. Meyer's programs and this exciting book.

Toshio Sumino, business owner

Homer Rice calls Paul J. Meyer a "coach of coaches," but Paul is a "coach of players," also. He was a motivational coach for me during my 12 years as a Pro with Detroit and Cleveland. I listened to his motivational recordings constantly. He has continued to be helpful in my life after football. As a leader of our sports ministry, to city wides, prisons, youth at risk, and in schools, his help has been invaluable. When I think of Paul J. Meyer, I think of a giver ... but not just of his money. He gives what all true coaches give — motivation, inspiration, and direction! He draws the best out of coaches and everyone he touches. This book is a boiled down, hard hitting, power packed version of his best jewels of wisdom. All coaches must read and apply its message. But, so should everyone.

Bill Glass, football coach

Contents

Dedication

This book was written specifically for the members of AFCA out of my profound respect for Grant Teaff and Homer Rice.

It isn't every day that you can connect with men of such caliber. I first met Homer Rice in 1966 when he and I did a seminar for coaches. We've been friends and encouragers of each other's dreams ever since.

Grant Teaff is also an incredible encourager and believer in others. He is, after all, a coach at heart! Everyone associated with the AFCA is fortunate to have Grant at the helm.

It is an honor to play a part in both of these great men's lives, and as a result, to play a part in your life as well. It is my hope that what you are about to read will encourage, challenge, and motivate you to reach your full potential as a person and as a coach.

That is my life's passion, and as coaches, that is what you do as well! My hat is off to you, fellow coaches, for what you do and what you make of young people today! You all are coaches and "builders of men," which makes you twice the leader!

The quotes of many great coaches are on the bottom of the pages that follow, but the list of great coaches is by no means exhaustive:

Paul Brown	Mack Brown
Frank Broyles	Bear Bryant
John Cooper	Don Coryell
Duffy Daugherty	Paul Dietzel
Bobby Dodd	Vince Dooley
Don Faurot	Hayden Fry
Joe Gibbs	Bill Glass
George Halas	Woody Hayes
John Heisman	Lou Holtz
Jimmy Johnson	Frank Kush
Tom Landry	Vince Lombardi
John Madden	Bill McCartney
Don Nehlen	Chuck Noll
Ara Parseghian	Joe Paterno
Dan Reeves	Homer Rice
Eddie Robinson	Knute Rockne
Darrell Royal	Erk Russell
Bo Schembechler	Don Shula
Steve Spurrier	Gene Stallings
Ron Stolski	Hank Stram
Fran Tarkenton	Grant Teaff
Bud Wilkinson	Gordon Wood
Bill Yeoman	Bob Zuppke

To every coach reading this book ... keep up the great work as builders of men!

— Paul J. Meyer

Foreword by Grant Teaff

Before I say anything, I want you to know that this is no ordinary author and this is no ordinary book. Paul J. Meyer is, as Homer Rice so aptly puts it, "The coach of coaches."

This book contains more than meets the casual eye! You should know that Paul J. Meyer has sold more than $2 billion worth of his programs and trainings over the years, and the backbone for most of those programs is what you are about to read!

The 5 Goals of Leadership have been proven to work, time and time again, in the lives of millions of people around the world. It's like the playbook that continues to get you back in the national championship games. Wouldn't you use it again and again? You bet!

Also, what you are about to read must be read more than once if you want to drive these principles deep into your heart and mind. The best trained team usually wins, and the same applies to you, as the coach.

I've had the privilege of working on various projects with Paul J. Meyer. He is who he says he is, and much more! He is a man whose life, practices, and principles are worth studying and copying! You will win as a result.

— Grant Teaff, Executive Director of AFCA

Preface by Homer Rice

I've been studying leadership principles since I was 12 years old. That means I have more than 65 years of experience under my belt, but in all my studying, watching, and learning of leadership, I've never found anyone who could break it down into understandable, bite-size pieces like Paul J. Meyer.

Paul J. Meyer is a giant and pioneer in the leadership industry. He knows how — as I've found from studying his materials — to not only teach a principle, but to also enable you to assimilate that principle into your own life. In other words, he changes your life.

To me, that's what it's all about. Making an impact and changing lives for the better, that excites and motivates me!

As a coach, you have a great responsibility to the young people you are leading. No doubt you already know that, but have you stopped to consider just how many people you are leading? You are leading: the team, the staff, the administration at the school, the alumni, the teachers, the fans, and the media.

You could be leading 50,000 to 1,000,000 people!

Use your time and influence wisely, and use the principles you gain from this book to make an even bigger impact in your arena.

— *Homer Rice*

Chapter 1
— *Just Rise to the Occasion*

On Rising to the Occasion:

"The difference between a successful person and others is not a lack of strength, not a lack of knowledge, but rather a lack of will."

— *Vince Lombardi*

Just Rise to the Occasion

Becoming a leader is always a choice, just as becoming a coach is a choice. Those who choose to become leaders will always find a way to rise to the occasion and become the coach they were meant to be.

As a result, doors of opportunity open wide to them. Growth and benefits come their way. They become better people, more confident, more capable, and higher paid! They make a greater impact in the lives of their players and the results are visible for all to see, both on and off the field.

> "Rise to the occasion! It is worth it in every way."
> — Paul J. Meyer

Unfortunately, not everyone will choose to rise to the occasion. In business, we see or experience the results: downsizing, layoffs, and capsizing every day. In families, we see or experience the results: abuse, divorce, and even murder. In politics, we see or experience the results: corruption, overspending, and broken promises. And in sports, you know what goes on behind closed doors.

On the Will to Win:

"It's not the size of the dog in the fight, but the size of the fight in the dog."
— Bear Bryant

The need for leadership is evident in every aspect of society. When we stand up and choose to become the leader we were meant to be, the tide begins to turn. In business, we see or experience the results — successful businesses, growth, and increased opportunity. In families we see or experience the results — love, peace, and order. In politics, we see or experience the results — strength, prosperity, and freedom. And in sports, we see the incredible results on and off the field!

> "We should endeavor to do something so that we may say that we have not lived in vain, that we may leave some impress of ourselves on the sands of time."
> — *Napoleon Bonaparte*

John F. Kennedy wisely noted, "Our problems are man-made ... therefore, they can be solved by man." I believe that many of today's problems can be solved by people rising to the occasion and becoming the leader they were meant to be. Choose to become the coach you were meant to be!

Anyone can be a leader

I often hear people debate leadership by asking, "Are leaders born or do they become leaders?" They take sides and try to prove their point, but the bottom line to me is this: *Who is going to fix the problem?*

On Taking Action:

"When all is said and done, more is said than done. Make it happen!"
— *Fran Tarkenton*

I don't care what someone has been taught or what the current philosophy says. I want results.

Debating something is only valuable if someone is willing to step forward and take action. Leaders are willing to change and bring about change. Anyone who rises to the occasion like this is a leader. Therefore, **I firmly believe that anyone can be a leader if he or she chooses to be.**

The fact is, each of us must rise up and become a leader. If we don't, we will always be subject to the whims, wishes, and wants of others. We will be taking orders instead of charting our own course toward success.

Vince Lombardi says it well, "Leaders aren't born, they are made. And they are made just like anything else, through hard work. And that's the price we'll have to pay to achieve that goal, or any goal."

The role of a leader

Some leaders step forward, rise to the occasion, and make things happen. They take responsibility and find answers, but what is their role?

In most environments, the organization is shaped like a pyramid, with upper-level executives at the top and everyone else on the bottom.

The boss who refuses to listen to anyone's advice is a perfect bad

---

On Eliminating Mistakes:

"Coaching is nothing more than eliminating mistakes before you get fired."

— *Lou Holtz*

---

example. Sadly, this is what often happens when leaders mentally put themselves at the top of the pyramid. This breeds nothing but trouble.

Since the real role of a leader is that of a servant, this  means that the pyramid should be "inverted."

People should be put on top and leaders should be put at the bottom. From this position, leaders are able to push their knowledge and expertise *up* the organization rather than letting it trickle *down*. They make things happen, they take responsibility, and they do everything that seasoned leaders do ... all with the understanding that their role is that of a servant.

When you turn it upside down, each element of the inverted pyramid is free to lead itself. Rather than having the head coach provide leadership from the top of the pyramid, the team provides leadership from all levels.

Some look at the inverted pyramid and think, "Yeah, those lousy leaders. They need to be at the bottom and serve me!" But having leaders at the bottom is not a slap in the face for leaders. Instead, it is time for everyone else to answer:

- **Will I rise to the occasion and lead?**

- **Will I take responsibility?**

On Controlling Your Destiny:

"Through the power of the mind, we can control our destiny."

— *Homer Rice*

- **Will I do what it takes to accomplish a given task?**

- **Will I serve others?**

For many, answering these questions will reveal that they need to become better leaders themselves. No more pointing fingers at imperfect bosses or coaches! Rising to the occasion is a personal choice that forces people to improve.

Coaches are serving their team, their assistants, their employees, their fans, and (for many) their schools by causing everyone to assume a greater position of leadership.

Choose to step forward and become a coach ... a *better coach* ... a *servant coach*. Perhaps author and business guru Peter Drucker summed it up best when he said, *"Leadership is not role, privilege, title, or money. It is responsibility."*

Why become a leader?

I assume you are a leader and aspiring to become a better coach or you wouldn't be reading this book. Why would you consider becoming a better leader and a better coach?

The answer is this: *to gain a benefit or avoid a loss.* Everything in life is done to gain a benefit or avoid a loss, and when it comes to choosing to be a better coach, this is most certainly true!

On Making a Difference:

"If you choose a life in coaching, you choose to try to make a difference in the lives of the people you come in contact with."

— *Ron Stolski*

The most tangible, hands-on reason for choosing to be a leader and a better coach: *You will make more money!*

For example, those who are leaders in business, sports, and Hollywood earn far more than those who are average — *even good* — at what they do. Leaders simply make more money, period. That is just the way it is. They probably didn't make that much money when they first began, but leaders will always rise to the top, eventually making the bigger incomes.

Another powerful reason for becoming a leader and better coach is *a strong internal desire to improve*. If you increase a skill by a mere 1%, you will find yourself miles ahead of the nearest competition. A 5% or 10% skill increase is off the charts! *How much room for improvement do you have as a coach? How strongly do you want to become a better person?*

> "To be able to lead others, a man must be willing to go forward alone."
> — *Harry Truman*

Others step forward and become leaders in order *to avoid a loss*. Imagine this scenario: Tell your team that you are going to cut half of the positions in 30 days and see what they will do! Can you imagine the incentive to step forward, to change, and to do anything that is required! Suddenly the fear of loss would cause players to do what they had previously chosen not to do. They would dig deep! They would set records! They would do the impossible!

On Teaching:

"It's not what you know, it's what you teach."
— *Bobby Dodd*

You need to see leadership the same way! Honestly, it is a choice that really is not that difficult to make. The end results will make it tremendously worth it, and it all begins with a choice.

How to become a leader and better coach

Becoming a leader and better coach cannot come by either getting a higher education or by adopting a dictator-like approach with people. Developing personality traits, like charisma and charm, aren't the answers either.

The way to become a leader and the best possible coach — *the coach you were meant to be* — is to follow these five steps until they become habits:

STEP #1 — **Define the specific results you wish to achieve.**

STEP #2 — **Create a plan that, when followed, will achieve those results.**

STEP #3 — **Develop the internal motivation necessary to take action.**

On Working Hard:

"I've had smarter people around me all my life, but I haven't run into one yet that can outwork me. And if they can't outwork you, then smarts aren't going to do them much good. That's just the way it is. And if you believe that and live by it, you'd be surprised at how much fun you can have."

— *Woody Hayes*

17

STEP #4 — **Build strong confidence within yourself and your team so that everyone performs at the optimum level.**

STEP #5 — **Instill a focused determination within your team so everyone can overcome problems and obstacles without giving up.**

No great coach can be truly great without consistently and habitually practicing these five steps. Yes, it will take time and effort to master these steps, but you can do it.

You can become the coach that you were meant to be ... if you choose to.

On the Last Lap:

"The hardest portion of any job or goal usually occurs in the second half. In sports, the fourth quarter, the ninth inning, and the last two minutes are all about 'finishing the job.'"

— Grant Teaff

On Finishing Well:

"I firmly believe that any man's finest hour, the greatest fulfillment of all that he holds dear, is that moment when he has worked his heart out in a good cause and lies exhausted on the field of battle — victorious."

— *Vince Lombardi*

Chapter 2
— *Because You Can!*

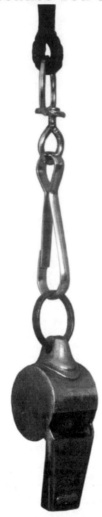

On Preparing to Win:

"The will to win is important, but the will to pre-pare is vital."

— *Joe Paterno*

Because You Can!

Many years ago, a 15-year old boy named John Goddard made a list of all the things he wanted to do in his lifetime. When he had finished the list, he had 127 items that became the blueprint for his life. Some of his earlier accomplishments were relatively common — become an Eagle Scout, learn to type 50 words a minute, and study jujitsu.

Other goals Goddard set were a little more unusual — milk a rattlesnake, read the entire encyclopedia, and make a parachute jump. Then there were goals that the average person might see as utterly impossible — climb Mt. Everest, visit every country in the world, and go to the moon.

Now for the amazing part of the story: By age 47, John Goddard had accomplished 103 items on his original list of 127!

Goddard was motivated to identify important dreams and begin working on them after hearing many older people say, "If only I had done this" or "If only I had done that when I was younger." He realized that too many people miss all the

On Determination:

"Show me someone who has done something worthwhile, and I'll show you someone who has overcome adversity."

— *Lou Holtz*

fun, excitement, and thrills of life because they do not plan ahead. *Making his list* was the beginning of his success.

Becoming a leader requires vision

The 127 items on John Goddard's list became his vision for the future. You have your own unique list or vision for the future, as does every leader, but there is one commonality among all lists, all visions, and all leaders.

That one common denominator is this: *the desire to succeed.*

> "What lies behind us and what lies before us are tiny matters compared to what lies within us."
> — Ralph Waldo Emerson

Everyone wants to succeed. That's a given! Nobody would purposefully set out to fail, but you would be surprised at how many people do just that. They want success, but they really don't know how to succeed.

Leaders understand success to be the progressive realization of worthwhile, predetermined personal and professional goals.

It takes time to accomplish specific goals, and leaders accept that. Great coaches know that from experience. They follow a lifelong process of setting goals and then achieving those goals.

This kind of success does not come by accident. Although many worthwhile achievements come as side

On Making Mistakes:

"Football is a game of errors. The team that makes the fewest errors in a game usually wins."

— *Paul Brown*

effects of some other purpose, they are, nevertheless, a direct consequence of the pursuit of predetermined goals. You cannot always foresee the ultimate effect of reaching a specific goal, but the important point to recognize is that achievement comes as a direct consequence of moving yourself and your organization toward predetermined goals.

An incident in the life of inventor Thomas A. Edison is a good example of how a predetermined goal resulted in an unanticipated accomplishment. While Edison was working on the telephone, he had an idea for producing a machine that would record and play back the human voice. He hastily drew a sketch, handed it to one of his laboratory assistants, and said, "Build one of these."

That machine became the first phonograph, the forerunner of all the sophisticated recording devices we enjoy today. Edison's invention grew out of its relationship to a totally different problem he had set out to solve. But, had he not been working toward a predetermined goal, this invention would not have been visualized.

Leaders and great coaches also succeed because they habitually follow the five important steps of leadership:

> "Keep away from people who try to belittle your ambitions. Some people always do that; but the really great make you feel that you too, can become great."
> — Mark Twain

On Teamwork:

"The leader starts with 'I' and ends up in 'we.' The team does it."
— Homer Rice

STEP #1:
Crystallize your thinking

The first step involves crystallizing your thinking so that you know where you stand now and where you want yourself and your organization to go. Remember, you will never reach goals by stumbling on them in the dark. You need a well-lit path and a well-conceived plan.

Developing a mission, vision, and purpose for yourself and your team is critically important. Just as you and your family would not begin a vacation trip without a clear destination in mind, leadership also begins with a clear idea of where you are going and why.

To crystallize your list and your vision, you must write it down. Since your vision is simply a picture of a desired future, it is important that you describe it by writing it down. John Goddard wrote down 127 items on his initial list. You must do the same. Start by writing down what it is you want to accomplish.

STEP #2:
Put your plan of action in writing

The second step toward becoming a better leader and better coach is to create a written plan for achieving your goals, along with deadlines for their attainment. It is extremely important that this plan is a written one, otherwise

On Influence:

"Other than my mom and dad, the people who had the most influence on me were my football coaches."

— *Dan Reeves*

what seems crystal clear today may easily become vague or forgotten in the urgency of tomorrow's affairs. Written goals keep you and your team on track, eliminating outside distractions and interruptions.

Additionally, written goals serve as a point of reference and a reminder of your objective. A written plan for achieving your own personal goals also conserves time and energy because you always know where you want to go. Deciding which step you want to take next is easy.

Setting a deadline for achieving your goal is extremely important. When you set a deadline, you act on the deadline because the deadline acts on you, alerting your body chemistry to react to the timetables you have set. As a consequence, you think, act, and react with appropriate energy and urgency.

> "The future belongs to those who believe in the beauty of their dreams."
> — *Eleanor Roosevelt*

Just as your muscles react in one particular way when you stoop to pick up the morning paper, and then react in an entirely different manner when you lift a 100-pound barbell, so does your mind prepare your body and attitude for responding appropriately to the deadlines you have set.

Deadlines create a challenge, and you will find yourself responding to that challenge. In football, the tension mounts as time runs out. The most exciting plays are often in the last two minutes, especially if the score is close, because

On Loving the Players:

"Coaching is a profession of love. You can't coach people unless you love them."
— *Eddie Robinson*

people respond in dramatic fashion to the challenge of deadlines.

Deadlines also help you maintain a positive mental attitude. Deadlines focus attention and concentration on the key objectives at hand. They enable you to eliminate distractions and to think clearly and creatively. You may have noticed that busy people are more positive than those who are idle. Physically and mentally, you are stimulated by the creative activity necessary to reach the deadlines you have set.

Deadlines must, of course, be handled with mature understanding. You are the master; the deadline is not the master. Sometimes through miscalculation or unforeseen circumstances, you will not reach a certain goal by the deadline you have set, but since you set your own deadlines, you can change them. You can reset your sights and change a deadline without abandoning the goal.

> **"Whatever you vividly imagine, ardently desire, sincerely believe, and enthusiastically act upon ... must inevitably come to pass!"**
> — *Paul J. Meyer*

In developing a written plan for achieving your goals, *defining the obstacles and roadblocks that stand between you and the achievement of your objective* is of utmost importance.

This part of the process is not making up excuses for something you have not done, it is taking a realistic look at

On Getting Up Again:

"Failure is not getting knocked down, it's not getting up again."

— *Vince Lombardi*

what you can expect to encounter as you work toward achieving a particular goal.

STEP #3:
Create desire and passion

The third step involves the development of a sincere desire to achieve your goals. *A burning passion for achievement marks the difference between a real goal and a mere wish.* A wish or a daydream has no substance; it is vague, unformed, and unsupported by action.

Desire, on the other hand, puts action at the center of the plans you've made. *Without strong enough desire to produce action, you will achieve little, no matter how worthy the goal nor how workable the plan you've devised.*

All of us are born with the desire to achieve, but we are also the recipients of a great deal of conditioning. Some of us may have allowed the flow of creativity and desire to be cut off by outside circumstances and influences. When we rediscover the freshness, vitality, and enthusiasm of creativity and desire each of us possessed as a child, we are ready to achieve success.

Many people spend their lives dispensing effort in "minimum daily requirements," just like a dose of vitamins. They rarely exceed the minimum effort required to get by.

On Wanting to Fight:

"Football, in its purest form, remains a physical fight. As in any fight, if you don't want to fight, it's impossible to win!"

— *Bud Wilkinson*

On the other hand, leaders and great coaches have vast reserves of strength like that experienced by athletes who run until exhausted and then reach their "second wind." A sincere, burning desire for achievement triggers the willingness to capitalize on your full potential, and then passion propels you toward the achievement of your goals.

Successful coaches develop a genuine, driving passion for the achievement of personal and team goals. Without that passion, any coach is robbed of power, strength, and conviction. On the other hand, coaches who develop passion and channel their desire toward the achievement of specific goals find their effectiveness and efficiency markedly increased.

STEP #4:
Develop supreme confidence and trust

The fourth step is to develop supreme confidence in yourself and in your ability to achieve. For great coaches, nothing offers greater confidence than possessing a clear-cut knowledge of planned actions and knowing the order in which they should be taken. The mere existence of a written plan of action contributes immeasurably to your effectiveness as a coach.

The most important source of confidence you can have is knowing that you can make the necessary internal and

On Enjoying Your Influence:

"Revel in the success you have had because each one of you have touched a kid somewhere. How many kids have you influenced in your career?"

— *Mack Brown*

external changes that are needed for tangible goals to become a reality.

Leadership also includes developing confidence in your team. For many coaches, it is difficult to develop the supreme confidence that a certain goal can be accomplished because they often lack confidence in the ability of their team.

This is indeed a challenge, but just as personal growth and achievement come from altering basic attitudes and habits of thought, team growth and achievement come the same way.

Trusting those on your team to grow and change is an important stimulus for the team to actually grow and

> **"Great men are meteors designed to burn so that the earth may be lighted."**
> — *Napoleon Bonaparte*

change. This kind of confidence is built on a firm foundation of personal rapport that grows rapidly as you share knowledge and experiences. *To develop such rapport you must be personally involved with your team.*

When you know firsthand why a particular team member might be motivated to accomplish a particular task, you are far more confident and trusting than if you had merely assigned the task and then walked away.

Coaches can always gain a kind of after-the-fact knowledge by assigning work and watching the results, but personal experience — the kind of individual interaction that turns superficial knowledge into practical confidence and

On Recruiting:

"It is a fine thing to have ability, but the ability to discover ability in others is the true test."
— *Lou Holtz*

trust — comes only from subjecting yourself and your team to situations that require the exercise of innate full potential. Stressful experiences can be strong builders of confidence and trust.

STEP #5:
Foster commitment and responsibility

The fifth step is to develop a sincere commitment to follow through on your plan regardless of obstacles, criticism, or circumstances, and in spite of what others say, think, or do.

This commitment sets you apart from the mediocre multitudes of people, leaders, and coaches who yield to the pressure of society, the desire for acceptance, and the temptation to conform.

Ironclad commitment is not the same as stubbornness. It is, rather, the application of sustained effort, controlled attention, and concentrated energy. The development of commitment and the acceptance of personal responsibility for results are the hallmarks of your refusal to be dissuaded, sidetracked, or steered off course.

One of the techniques for developing this kind of commitment and determination is the use of the "act-as-if" principle. Begin to act as you will act when the goal is reached. Practice the attitudes and habits you have chosen to develop.

On Achieving Success:

"I don't know anyone who achieved success by himself. The ability to work with people and make them the best they can be comes from seasons in practice and in the game."

— *Dan Reeves*

We learn to do by doing. Act out the role you have chosen for yourself and believe in the possibility of reaching your goal. After all, the greatest motivator of all is belief.

The key to developing ironclad commitment lies in the acceptance of personal responsibility for your own success. *And as a leader and coach, you have the same commitment for your team's goals.* If you are going to be successful, it is your responsibility to see the process through.

> **"The greatest motivator of all is belief."**
> — Paul J. Meyer

The bottom line

These five steps are required to become a better leader and a better coach. As you work to make these steps natural and habitual parts of your life and leadership style, boldly review the bottom line and ask yourself:

- **Have I crystallized my thinking so that I know where I stand now and where I want to go? Are my vision, mission, and purpose clear?**

- **Do I have a detailed written plan to achieve each important goal, and is there a deadline for its achievement?**

- **Do I have a burning desire to achieve the goals I have set for myself?**

On Success:

"The difference between ordinary and extraordinary is that little extra."
— *Jimmy Johnson*

- **Do I have supreme confidence in myself and those on my team to reach our goal?**

- **Have I accepted personal responsibility for the success of the team and for the achievement of my own personal goals?**

- **Do I possess the iron-willed determination to follow through regardless of circumstances or what other people say, think, or do?**

Now it is time to take each step and become the coach that you were meant to be ... because you can!

On Reaping Your Rewards:

"All young coaches need to realize that some day, if they stay in this game and pursue their dream of being the best coaches they can be, they will also reap the rewards of all the years of effort, time, and hard work."

— *Grant Teaff*

On Coaching:

"All coaching is, is taking a player where he can't take himself."

— *Bill McCartney*

Chapter 3
STEP #1 – Crystallize Your Thinking

On Reaching Your Goals:

"Setting a goal is not the main thing. It is deciding how you will go about achieving it and staying with that plan."

— *Tom Landry*

STEP #1
Crystallize Your Thinking

W hat is it you really want? Do you know what you want or are you so busy dealing with daily concerns that you don't really know what you desire?

Most people are controlled by their day rather than rising up and taking control of their day. They are so busy rushing from one "top priority" to the next, putting out one fire after another, that they lose sight of their bigger goal.

Before long, they don't remember what it was that they really wanted, or even worse, they have given up on trying to reach their goals.

Great coaches, on the other hand, have learned how to regain their focus. They know how to get back in control. *The answer is to crystallize your thinking!* This begins when you

On Winning Close Games:

"The thing that means the most in football is winning the close games. The teams with the most impressive records in football aren't really all that dominant. They just win the close games. It's that kind of sport, and it's that way every year."

— *Don Coryell*

choose to become the coach you were meant to be and *clearly define your goals and objectives.*

Define your goals and objectives

Crystallized thinking begins when you identify the specific goals you want to achieve ... and identify where you and your team stand now in relation to those goals and objectives.

If you must stop to ask for directions, would you ask a tourist or a local? Obviously, you want a local to give you directions because you want to reach your destination. The local knows where you are and can give you clear directions to where you want to go.

> "I have fought a good fight, I have finished my course, I have kept the faith."
> — II Timothy 4:7

The same holds true for your pursuit of success as a coach. When you know exactly where you are and you know where you want to go, you are ready to take the next step in the right direction.

Crystallized thinking is like a map. At its core is simply the act of clearly defining your goals and objectives. *If you are dissatisfied with your present rate of progress compared to your true potential for success, your goals are not clearly defined.* Every achievement is based upon that simple comparison. Every achievement begins with the knowledge of current status and eventual destination.

On Losing:

"Losing a game is heartbreaking. Losing your sense of excellence or worth is a tragedy."
— *Joe Paterno*

To help you define your goals and objectives, answer the following questions:

WHAT DO YOU WANT?

Clarify your personal dreams. What is it that you want so badly? And as a coach, what is it you want your team to accomplish? What is the end result you seek? Your answer will help you crystallize your thinking.

As a coach, you must know precisely what you want.

WHY DO YOU WANT IT?

Do you know why you want what you want? When you discover the true motivation behind your specific dreams and desires, your quest for success has real meaning. From a personal and leadership position, this information is vital.

As a coach, you must know why you do what you do ... because it will motivate you!

WHY DO YOU NOT ALREADY HAVE IT?

If a certain goal is important to you and/or your team, why is the goal not already a reality? Is it because you lack a specific skill? Capability? Motivation? What has kept you

On Coaching Successfully:

"The secret of coaching success can be reduced to a simple formula: strict discipline in your training program and on the field, combined with a high and continuing interest in all your other relationships with your kids."

— *Knute Rockne*

37

from achieving the goal before now? Your answer might very well be *the* answer to reaching your goal!

As a coach, you must honestly and consistently measure, track, and manage your progress.

WHAT ARE THE BENEFITS?

Will you benefit by reaching the desired goal? Will your team benefit? Additionally, do you know what those precise benefits will be? Self-motivation comes much more quickly when everyone understands clearly how they will benefit. Make sure the benefits are always in front of you and your team.

As a coach, keeping the vision and the benefits in front of your team is both necessary and incredibly beneficial!

HOW WILL YOU KNOW WHEN YOU GET IT?

This might seem like a silly question, but it is important that you are able to actually measure your success. This includes measuring your growth as a coach. If a win-loss statement doesn't give you enough information, perhaps a points scored/points missed statement or even a correct play call/incorrect play call statement is the way to know when you have reached your goal and/or are succeeding in your leadership position.

On Being Practical:

"A philosophy is an abstract statement on what you believe. It doesn't say how you are going to do it."

— *Gene Stallings*

As a coach, you must pay close attention to your goals every step of the way.

WHERE WILL IT LEAD YOU?

You have a well-defined goal and you are making significant progress toward it. Has anything changed since you started? Has the team improved beyond your goal? Is hitting your goal still where you want to end up? Perhaps you've realized that your goal is not as big as you thought it was.

As a coach, your attention to detail will enable you to alter your course before your initial goal takes you some place you don't intend to go.

Develop a crystallized mission

Now that you have defined your goals and objectives, it is time to define your mission. Whether for yourself or for your team, a mission statement is *a brief but powerful summary of your reason for existing*. It provides direction, focus, and consistency in everything you do.

The sheer act of crystallizing your thinking can generate tremendous excitement and enthusiasm, but those effects are temporary. Once they wear off, a solid mission statement will help keep everyone on track toward the objectives you have set. Part of your job as a coach is to keep the momentum moving forward; so allowing the excitement and enthusiasm to wear off is never an option.

On What's Needed:

"Morale and attitude are the fundamental ingredients to success."

— *Bud Wilkinson*

A crystallized mission requires that you write it down. *If you fail to write down your mission statement, you will get lost along the way.* That is just the way it is.

A mission statement is only effective if everyone knows and understands it! With many teams, the players never really grasp the meaning of the team mission statement. When that is the case, the coach is at fault.

The lack of understanding will hurt your team's efforts, while a clear understanding will benefit your team. Work to make your mission statement as clear and brief as possible because it must be understood, accepted, internalized, and memorized by everyone on your team. **As a coach, this is of paramount importance!**

To craft a well-written mission statement, you need to remember specifically what it is you are trying to accomplish. With that in mind, state why you exist: *Why are you doing what you are doing?*

Perhaps your goal is to make a six-figure income and you want this goal to become a reality so that you can provide for your family (i.e. quit your second job, provide for other family members, meet your family investment goals, etc.).

Perhaps your goal is to win a district championship, national championship, or the Super Bowl. Whatever your

On Listening to Your Team:

"If you can get the team talking to you, that is important because in coaching, so often, we talk too much and don't listen. Same thing goes with head coaches working with our assistants. You had better listen. You don't have to take the advice, but it does not hurt to listen."

— *Mack Brown*

reason, it is *your reason* for doing what you do. That is your mission.

But as a coach, you are also leading other people, which means they have goals and dreams that they want to accomplish. When they reach their goals, you reach your goals, which is a positive by-product of setting and reaching goals.

With that said, you must have a team mission that includes everyone on the team. It will take time and effort to capture the thoughts and ideas of every member, but the result will be greater dedication and involvement from every individual. Great coaches listen to everyone on the team!

> **"If you are not now making the progress you would like to make and are capable of making, it is simply because your goals are not clearly defined."**
> — *Paul J. Meyer*

By paying close attention to each member, you can chart a course that will closely parallel the dreams and desires of everyone on the team. People who are excited to be "part of the team" are not only dedicated to the group's mission, but they also are happy to be there because their own goals are being accomplished.

A leader with great vision but no followers ... *is not really a leader*. Similarly, though a coach without a great vision is still a coach, he is not a great coach! The clearer the

On Conditioning:

"You can control what comes into your mind, and as a result, control your actions. You can become the person and leader you want to be."
— *Homer Rice*

41

mission statement for you and everyone on the team, the closer everyone is to success.

Create a crystallized vision

A mission statement states why you exist, while a vision statement *tells everyone where you are going*. The vision statement therefore is crucial to your success, individually and as a team.

For you, *crystallizing your vision makes the process of becoming an effective coach much easier*. For your team, a concise vision identifies your overall goals and links their goals to yours.

Without a vision statement, many on your team are likely to feel that they are a part of something small and ordinary. The vision statement sets the tone for future growth and should be exciting but brief. It should convey a sense of urgency and a clear sense of destiny!

A vision statement defines the future; every day you work without it, you are working for yesterday rather than for tomorrow. Your vision statement should be a conduit or channel for your goals and expectations. It should challenge you

On Building Confidence:

"Find the method that will make it work; then you have something to make it go. Now, players may not understand, even at the pro level, exactly what you are doing. But the fact that you are doing something, the fact that you are creating philosophy in there, they know you have something going. That's very important in giving the team confidence."

— *Tom Landry*

and your team to a bright new future without burdening anyone with the mistakes and poor choices that may have been made in the past.

While a mission statement is largely a consensus of crystallized thinking, a vision statement may not require input from every member of your team. *You, as the coach, are the individual who should determine (or at least help determine) what the future holds for your team.*

Truly successful coaches know where their team is headed. Their crusade focuses on leading the team along that predetermined pathway to success.

Your vision statement tells the world what you intend to do with the gifts and talents your Creator has given you and your team.

Define your crystallized purpose

With a mission statement, you said why you exist. With a vision statement, you said where you are going. *Now it is time to tell why you are doing what you are doing.*

Naturally, the "why" for doing things is part of what personally motivates you. You might be thinking, "Shouldn't I know my purpose, my why for doing something, *before* I create a mission or vision statement?" Yes, you should. *The motivation for action always precedes the action itself.*

So why save the statement of purpose for last? Largely because it requires the highest degree of deliberate, planned, crystallized thinking. You, and everyone on your team, must

On Using Your Head:

"Football is a game played with arms, legs, and shoulders but mostly from the neck up."
— *Knute Rockne*

individually answer this question: **"Why am I doing what I'm doing?"**

State your purpose briefly and clearly. All combined, your mission statement, vision statement, and purpose statement, should be less than 100 words.

Your future with crystallized thought

If you want to reach your full individual and team potential for success, then clear and concise mission, vision, and purpose statements are essential.

> **"Written plans minimize the tendency to procrastinate."**
> — *Paul J. Meyer*

Why? *Because crystallized thought motivates action.* The only way to succeed long term is to have your thoughts crystallized. Your mission, vision, and purpose statements are just that — crystallized thought.

Remember, if you are not making the progress you would like to make and are capable of making, it is simply because your goals are not clearly defined.

Crystallize your thinking today ... so that your future becomes what you want it to be!

On Statistics:

"Statistics always remind me of the fellow who drowned in a river where the average depth was only three feet."

— *Woody Hayes*

44

On Football:

"Football isn't a contact sport, it's a collision sport. Dancing is a contact sport."

— *Duffy Daugherty*

Chapter 4
STEP #2 — Put Your Plan of Action in Writing

On Big Dreams:

"Big dreams create the magic that stir men's souls to greatness."

— *Bill McCartney*

STEP #2
Put Your Plan of Action in Writing

With your thinking crystallized, you know exactly what you want. You know your personal and team goals and objectives. The next step is to write a plan of action to take you there.

Written plans are essential if you intend to push your goal beyond the realm of daydreaming. With plans clearly detailed and carefully drawn, you cut through any confusion your own thought process may have created.

This is a critical time to follow through because power comes from writing down your plans. Don't miss out! Written plans allow you to convert theory into practice, thought into action, and dreams into reality.

On Listening to Gossip:

"You're never as good as everyone tells you when you win, and you're never as bad as they say when you lose."

— *Lou Holtz*

The power of written plans

Plans have a way of creating "inspirational discontent" with things as they are. You become dissatisfied with the status quo and so you work to make your plans an actual reality.

Your energy level is up, you are excited, and you cannot help but be enthusiastic. *Rather than wondering when or if you should start, you can hardly wait to begin.*

Written plans have the power to really move you! *But, if you are unable to write down your goal, that goal may never become a reality.* Written plans for achieving goals are a necessity. Typically, written plans contain these five essential elements:

1. *The goal* written in a clear and concise manner

2. *A target date* for the achievement of the goal

3. *A summary of benefits to be gained and losses to be avoided* as a result of achieving the goal

4. *A summary of possible obstacles* to achievement, along with written strategies for overcoming these roadblocks

5. *A step-by-step plan* for the achievement process

On What It Takes:

"Do what's right, treat other people like you want to be treated, and give me 110 percent."
— *Don Nehlen*

Seeing the big picture

Let me take a moment to possibly challenge your thinking. It's great that you have a goal that you are working toward, but what good is reaching a goal if you abandon everything else in life?

Granted, I don't know what your goals are, but I do know that many coaches become consumed with their goals. They know how to chart a course that will take them straight to their desired goals.

There is, of course, nothing wrong with hitting your goals, but is it really necessary to neglect your health to achieve a certain goal? Is it really necessary to abuse people to achieve a goal? Is it really necessary to neglect your family so you can achieve a goal? I agree that it is

> **"Plans are only good intentions unless they immediately degenerate into hard work."**
> — *Peter Drucker*

vitally important that you reach your goals, but I would like to add, "in every area of life."

Truly great coaches will achieve their specific goals *as they work to achieve their full potential*. What is their full

On Family:

"As I look back now on my coaching career, I think of my family; I think of the days that we spent together. I say this to coaches everywhere: If you ever have a chance to take your kids with you, take them. Don't miss that opportunity. Because when it's all over and done with, when you look back, those are going to be your fondest memories."

— *John Madden*

potential? It is setting and striving to achieve goals in all six key areas of life. Those who focus solely on one goal to the detriment of all the other areas of life might end up being incredible in that one area, but they are lopsided in every other area!

How do you explain the unhappiness of some wealthy people? How do you explain why a famous person would commit suicide? Why do the powerful often take what is not theirs? Money, fame, and power cannot satisfy.

The secret to true success, as all truly great coaches know, is to set goals in *ALL* six key areas of life. That includes:

1) *Family/Home* — These goals affect you and those you love. They are usually goals that guide your inter-action and define your commitment toward those you care about.

2) *Financial/Career* — These goals affect earnings, sav-ings, and investments, and govern how you earn, acquire, and use financial leverage. Financial and career goals also relate to business advancement and contribution, as well as to your personal legacy to those you love.

3) *Mental/Educational* — These goals guide you toward intellectual pursuits and help you experience the true joy of learning.

On Being Consistent:

"Be consistently good before you can be great."
— *Mack Brown*

4) Physical/Health — These goals deal with your overall health and fitness.

5) Social/Cultural — These goals help you engage in different experiences, meet new people, and accept new challenges of interacting with others, thus strengthening your ability to interact personally with others.

6) Spiritual/Ethical — These goals affect your relationship with your Creator and tie you to certain ethical standards of moral behavior and conduct.

I don't believe that anyone, *regardless of lifestyle or status,* is a complete success unless he or she has developed significant goals in each of these six areas of life.

Likewise, you cannot be a truly great coach until you have developed significant goals in each of these six areas of life. It therefore goes without saying that achieving lasting success, personally and as a coach, requires balance.

Where balance begins

One of the easiest ways to conceptualize the six areas of life is to think of the spokes in a wheel. Each spoke runs

On Coaching:

"Bear Bryant's Three Rules for coaching:
#1 — Surround yourself with people who can't live without football.
#2 — Recognize winners. They come in all forms.
#3 — Have a plan for everything."
— *Bear Bryant*

from the center of the wheel (the center of your life) out to the rim. And, very importantly, all the spokes are the same length. Such a wheel would look like this:

TOTAL PERSON®

Financial & Career

Family & Home

Mental & Educational

YOU

Spiritual & Ethical

Physical & Health

Social & Cultural

Copyright © 1960 Paul J. Meyer

If the spokes were different lengths, however, the wheel might resemble an egg, a triangle, or even a half-moon, which doesn't make for a smooth ride!

On Team Goals:

"If a team is to reach its potential, each player must be willing to subordinate his personal goals to the good of the team."

— *Bud Wilkinson*

Most likely, given a lack of focus on one or more areas, some spokes in your life are longer than others. This means that to some degree or another, your wheel is lopsided. This is inefficient at best, dangerous at worst.

Those who are severely lopsided and do not pause long enough to correct their wheel (balance their lives) are in trouble. All forward motion, be it in their personal goals or coaching efforts, will eventually grind to a halt. It is inevitable.

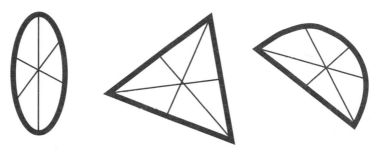

To become the coach you are capable of becoming, each spoke of your wheel (each of the six areas of life) must be adequately balanced.

Slow down to speed up

You have heard it said that there are times in your life when the only way to speed up is to first slow down. A simple example is passing a test to become certified. You slow

On Being Honest:

"I'm not trying to win a popularity poll. I'm trying to win football games. I don't like nice people. I like tough, honest people."

— *Woody Hayes*

down to study and pass the test, then you can go faster with your new skills and certification.

The same slow-down-to-speed-up concept applies to living a balanced life, but most people say they are too busy to pause long enough to even get a view of the six areas of life, let alone stop to set goals in each area.

Would you not agree that a round wheel is the best option?

Finding that balance is the goal. Being too busy cannot be the answer. Those who are too busy to correct their lopsided lives have not stopped to consider their faulty logic. They are lopsided and therefore inefficient, yet they are too busy to fix what ails them. That might be true for the next 24 hours, but what about the next 24 months or even 24 years?

Over time, a lopsided person will be passed by virtually everyone! It's the tortoise and the hare all over again. The answer is to slow down so that you can speed up.

I challenge you to take the time now to start working on finding balance in your life. Balance does not come instantly and neither is it a one-time thing. You will have to constantly adjust, but that is the reality of achieving balance in life.

The best place to begin is with a personal assessment. Where do you stand now in each of the six areas of life? If "10" represents perfection and "1" means you have neglected this area, where would you rank yourself? Where would you mark your progress in each area of life?

On the Little Things:

"In the successful organization, no detail is too small to escape close attention."

— *Lou Holtz*

Rank yourself at each level. If, for example, you feel you are an "8" in the Family/Home area of life, then put a mark in the "8" box. Do the same for each area.

	FAMILY/HOME	FINANCIAL/CAREER	MENTAL/EDUCATIONAL	PHYSICAL/HEALTH	SOCIAL/CULTURAL	SPIRITUAL/ETHICAL
10						
9						
8						
7						
6						
5						
4						
3						
2						
1						

How you rank yourself should be an honest reflection of where you feel you stand currently in relation to your potential for success.

Now, here is the test! Turn back to the Total Person® wheel and put a dot on each spoke that corresponds to the mark on the assessment chart on the previous page. A score of "5" would be a dot in the middle of a spoke and a perfect "10" would be a dot right on the rim.

Then, when you have all six dots on the wheel, starting clockwise connect the dots.

On Making It Happen:

"There's no substitute for guts."

— *Bear Bryant*

Is your wheel round? How fast do you think it can roll through life? Which areas of life need the most work? In which areas of life do you currently excel? In which area(s) could you create the greatest immediate impact? Which area(s) would take the most time to improve? What goals can you begin to achieve today that will contribute to a more rounded wheel?

Many coaches who have achieved extraordinary success in sports are dismayed to see that their own self-evaluation indicates a dramatic need for personal improvement. If this is true for you, you may find yourself feeling downcast, depressed, or even angry about where you stand in the other areas of life.

There's no need to feel dejected about the ranking(s) you have assigned to the various areas. Instead, turn negative emotion into a positive, productive passion — *a genuine enthusiasm for making appropriate changes.*

Use your assessment to grow!

Begin making significant changes by setting goals and priorities in each area of life. You will find even small changes significant and exciting! Then, develop the step-by-step plans necessary to guarantee the achievement of those goals. Once you have the plans in place, it's time to get into action to achieve the results you want.

On Facing Facts:

"Coaches have to watch for what they don't want to see and listen to what they don't want to hear."

— *John Madden*

Remember, 90% of all failure comes from quitting. The reverse is also true: You are 90% of the way to your goals the moment you commit yourself to their achievement.

Your conscious focus is determined by your subconscious intention. If you are sincerely focused on improving your standing in a certain area of life, you find that you begin paying attention to that area. Improvement will come!

Determining where you stand in each of the six areas of life may be a slightly painful process, but it is a necessary one if you are to give direction to your dreams. The process also can be an enjoyable one as you relive and

> **"Golf is the easy part. The hard part is trying to balance your life."**
> — *Tiger Woods*

recognize the success you've achieved so far in each area.

Gaining self-knowledge through this kind of self-examination process can also be extremely stimulating because you develop a well-balanced awareness of who you really are now. This is valuable information as you explore the kind of individual you wish to become.

All of us are tempted to keep doing the things we do best. This is because we all possess unique strengths and abilities that we enjoy using. However, we also have certain shortcomings and deficiencies that we often wish to ignore. To become the coach you were meant to be, you must recognize not only those talents and abilities you put on display,

On Winning:

"If winning isn't everything, why do they keep score?"

— *Vince Lombardi*

but also the hidden weaknesses that you seldom think about or admit.

The next step ... setting goals

With your assessment results in hand, you are ready to move ahead to set concrete goals in each of the six areas of life. This process demands that you decide what comes first, second, third, and so on. Your own values will serve to guide you in selecting those items that will have greatest priority for you.

Once you've established priorities, you will probably be able to picture the end result of achieving the goals you have set. This is a critical test, for without a clear mental picture, the results you obtain will likely be blurred or distorted — much like taking a picture with an out-of-focus camera.

There is no way to achieve a clear-cut goal unless you begin with a clear-cut mental picture of the results the goal will produce.

The goals you set in each area of life must meet five criteria to be considered true goals. Goals that don't meet these criteria are wishes, which are vague and unformed. Make sure your goals include these five criteria:

CRITERIA #1: **Goals must be written and specific.** William James told us more than a century ago that writing crystallizes thought and crystallized thought motivates action. If you find yourself unable to set

On People Liking You:

"If people like you too much, it's probably because they are beating you."

— *Steve Spurrier*

down a goal in writing and describe it in vivid detail, then your thinking about the goal is not crystal clear. Hazy goals produce, at best, hazy results. Typically, they produce no results at all!

CRITERIA #2: **The goals you set must be your own personal goals.** Of course, no one else can set goals for you because no one else has your particular view of what must be accomplished. Nor does anyone have your unique personality, abilities, needs, or potential for success. Seeking goals that have been set for you by others is tantamount to pursuing borrowed goals, and though they may be positive and productive in and of themselves, they can never generate the level of passion, desire, and determination required for you or anyone else to achieve them.

CRITERIA #3: **Your goals must be stated positively.** If you are able to form a clear mental picture of yourself taking some positive action, it is impossible to see yourself not doing something! Your goals must create

On the Coach's Wife:

"They talk about how hard coaches work. They work 18, 20 hours a day. They sleep on a couch. They don't come home. You know, that's not the hard job. The hard job is a coach's wife, believe me. The job of the coach's wife, she has to be mother, father, driver, doctor, nurse, coach, everything, because the coach is out there working."

— *John Madden*

a vivid mental image of you taking action to achieve them!

You may have noticed that some people set negative goals, such as, "I will not waste time" or "I will not be late." Their goals would work better if they were stated positively: "I will make productive use of my time" or "I will arrive at work on time."

CRITERIA #4: **Goals must be realistic and attainable.** This is not to say that goals you set in any area of life must be commonplace or ordinary. Indeed, *a mediocre goal will hold little motivation for you*, while a high goal can be reached easier than a low goal. A realistic goal represents an objective toward which you are willing and able to work.

The attainability of a goal, on the other hand, is a question best answered by the goal's unique timetable. Long-range goals often hold less motivation than short-range goals. The key to accomplishing long-range objectives, then, is to set intermediate steps that will keep you on track and give you confidence to continue on the journey. Goals that were unimaginable only days ago now move into view, and your new vantage point allows you to see greater opportunities to express your innate potential.

On Bigger Goals:

"If you're bored with life — *you don't get up every morning with a burning desire to do things* — you don't have enough goals."

— *Lou Holtz*

CRITERIA #5: **The goals you set must include personality changes.** This is not to say that every goal you write down must require you to change personally, but personality changes must be taken into account. Goals *to have* must also include goals *to become*. Set intangible goals of becoming (developing required personality characteristics) so you can then set goals of a more tangible nature.

The result of goals in each area of life

Setting and achieving goals in each area of life will make you a balanced person, truly capable of reaching your full potential! I call such a person a **Total Person**®. You are well-rounded (remember the wheel?) and on track to reach goals in each area of life. You are balanced. You are both a coach and a role model! You are poised to reach your full potential!

Becoming a Total Person® begins with these very important steps:

STEP #1 — Determine your most important objectives. What one thing would you like to see happen in each area of life? If one goal is especially important to you, put it at the top of your list.

Next, decide what comes second, third, fourth, and so on. Don't limit your imagination by taking into account the time, effort, or money required to make your vision a reality.

On Keeping Quiet:

"When you win, say nothing. When you lose, say less."

— Paul Brown

Concentrate on making a long list of goals for each area of life.

As you are writing, consider what you will need to do to reach a specific goal. For example, if one of your goals is to have a more meaningful impact in your players' lives, yet you don't have enough time to do it, then learning how to more effectively use your time would be a goal to write down as well. Place your goal to impact your players' lives in the Social/Cultural area and place your goal to more effectively use your time in the Mental/Educational area. ***Both goals are equally important.***

With each list per area, whether it is long or short, review every item and decide if what you have written is merely a wish or a serious goal. Is it something you really want or is it something you would like? Can you crystallize your thinking about the goal or does it remain vague?

Most wishes need to be set aside, although some can become actual goals if you choose to remove the mental road-blocks. It's up to you to decide if you want to pursue something or not.

Making your list may take some time, so take as long as you need and avoid the temptation to rush the job.

STEP #2 — Plan for achievement. With the serious goals that remain, make sure they are in the order in which you want to accomplish them. Repeat this ordering process

---

On What's Most Important:

"You will coach much better when you realize it is not about you. It is about the kids. All about the kids. You owe them your best every day."
— *Ron Stolski*

---

for each of the other five areas of life. The act of prioritizing your list brings incredible clarity and focus to your goals.

Also, having a prioritized list enables you as a coach to always remain on track. When one goal is reached, you move on to the next. You are never lost, wondering what to do next.

STEP #3 — Take daily action. Select the first goal from the top of a list in one area of life. Create a list of things you must do today to make progress toward that specific goal. Do this for every top item in each area of life.

The action steps you take today may seem small or relatively inconsequential, but don't let that stop you. As long as you move slightly forward every day, you will eventually reach every goal in each area of life.

What will your action steps be today? Maybe you want to read 15 minutes from a book on management or maybe you want to exercise for 30 minutes. Maybe you want to call someone you've been meaning to call or perhaps you can discuss certain plans with your team.

Whatever your goals, the important thing is to get up and take action right now!

Your goals need to be YOUR goals!

Are the goals you've written down for each of the six areas of life your own goals? They should be. No one else

On Life After the Game:

"The game covers only a short period of life, and then it's over. A player's life after football, and how he lives it, is more important."

— *Dan Reeves*

can decide which personal goals you should pursue. You and you alone must choose them for yourself.

A goal of your own will move you to take action! It will excite you! It will cause you to get up early and go to bed late! It will even keep you up at night! It will motivate you to overcome seemingly insurmountable odds!

Here are several real-life examples of goals that other people have set in each area of life:

Financial/Career:
- Increase income to $250,000 a year
- Recruit 20% more players
- Beat last year's endorsements by 50%

Family/Home:
- Move to a larger home
- Take the family to Hawaii for a week
- Enjoy a weekend away with spouse each quarter

Physical/Health:
- Learn CPR
- Weigh 180 pounds
- Work out three times per week

Social/Cultural:
- Join the AFCA

On Getting Better:

"We compete, not so much against an opponent, but against ourselves. The real test is this: Did I make my best effort on every play?"

— *Bud Wilkinson*

- Invite certain people to the games
- Spend more time with players

Mental/Educational:
- Listen to a CD on self-improvement daily
- Read a book on leadership daily
- Attend trainings that help the team

Spiritual/Ethical:
- Be at peace
- Double financial giving
- Read a chapter of scripture each day

Whatever the goal, make sure it is YOUR goal. You have no doubt noticed already that some goals fit into two or more areas of life. How do you handle this? Simply put the goals where you want to put them. It really makes no difference ... as long as you set goals and take action steps to reach those goals.

What balance brings to you

Setting and reaching goals in every area of life brings more your way than the accomplishment of one massive goal. Here is what balance brings to you:

On Life After Football:

"My best team will be the one that produces the best doctors, lawyers, fathers, and citizens, not necessarily the one with the best record."

— *Joe Paterno*

65

#1 — Drive, while not being driven: As you make progress toward your goals, you do not have to pressure yourself to accomplish every goal at the same time. That is not realistic. Instead, with careful planning, you can work on several goals at once. And when you accomplish one or more goals on your list, begin to focus on your other goals.

#2 — Awareness to keep you on track: Simply being aware of several goals at once can help ensure that you do not devote too much time to any one goal or any one area of life. The most important thing is not to try to reach each goal at the same time.

#3 — Clarity of purpose: With your goals listed in each area of life, you have incredible clarity of purpose. You know exactly what you want to do! Choosing which goal or goals to work on first is based on your wants and priorities. You are ready to go ... and you know where you are going!

#4 — Positive self-image: Knowing that you are on track to reach your goals has a way of producing in you a strong positive self-image. You can face tests and challenges because you know you are in control. Every step, even little steps, is a step in the right purposeful direction. It shows in your subconscious behavior and then in your actions. It eventually spills over into every area of your life.

On the Team:

"If you lose the game, it's the coach's fault. If you win the game, praise the players. That's the best way to do it."

— *Mack Brown*

Your self-image, or the mental picture you have of yourself, determines to a large extent the level of success you will reach, as a coach and as an individual. The more positive your self-image, the more opportunities you have to pursue success and the more you are able to overcome obstacles that stand in your way.

> **"In life, as in football, you won't go far unless you know where the goal posts are."**
> — *Arnold H. Glasgow*

#5 — **Self-reliance:** Being able to set and achieve goals will deepen your trust in yourself. You know you are capable of reaching goals, so you have more confidence in your actions.

#6 — **Increased creativity:** No greater exercise in creativity exists than setting goals in each area of life! It demands that you think "outside the box." As a result, you must be creative and devise your own path toward the achievement of your goals. Your creativity blossoms as a result.

#7 — **Unflinching resilience:** When you dare to be creative enough to plan your own destiny, you not only discover what works and what doesn't, but you also learn how to handle disappointment and self-doubt. *You become resilient!* Your successes in other areas of life help you rebound from temporary setbacks and failures. And when the going gets tough, you creatively think of other ways to reach your goals.

On Getting It Done:

"There is always a way."
— *Grant Teaff*

67

#8 — Encouragement for others: Because of what you have learned and have accomplished yourself, you are able to encourage others to do the same. People who are jealous and insecure cannot encourage, but you can genuinely encourage others to do what you have done. Your confidence mixed with your experience are greatly needed by those around you.

With all of these qualities at work in your life, you are not only a great coach, but you are an incredible role model. You are unique, rare, and worthy of being emulated.

Stop and think about it. How many people do you

> **"Coaches are role models."**
> — *Paul J. Meyer*

know who really are balanced *and* accomplishing their goals? How many people do you know who know exactly where they are going *and* can keep their creativity in the midst of setbacks? How many people do you know who are self-confident *and* who will encourage you at the same time?

Most likely, you can count them on one hand ... but you can be that rare person as you work to set and achieve your goals in all six areas of life!

On Hitting the Goal:

"Then somewhere along the line — and it couldn't have been until late in the season — we realized we had a chance to do something no one else had done: To win all the games. That became important, but if we had to lose, we wanted to make sure that it wasn't in the Super Bowl. If we ended 16-1, the season would have been a failure."

— *Don Shula*

On Direction:

"A strong commitment to your philosophy is about as important a thing as you can have. You've got to convince your people, your coaches, and your players, and then you've got to make it work."

— *Erk Russell*

Chapter 5
— *Self-Talk for Coaches*

On Belief:

"Life's battles don't always go to the stronger or faster man. But sooner or later the man who wins, is the man who thinks he can."

— Vince Lombardi

Self-Talk for Coaches

T ime out! We've covered a lot of ground to this point, but if you really wish to grasp, understand, internalize, and live what you have learned and will learn, then this chapter might be the most valuable chapter in the entire book!

What does success look like?

Think for a minute of the 10 most successful people you know. What qualities, traits, talents, and abilities do you see? What is it specifically that makes them successful?

What is interesting, in addition to what you see, is the amount of common ground between each successful person. Most of them are probably highly creative people. They exhibit a desire for achievement and accomplishment. They are decisive, action-oriented people. Some of them reached the pinnacle of success quickly and brilliantly. Others plodded with determination through a long period of gradual achievement until they reached the top.

In spite of all the differences you will note among successful people, one quality is always present — *winners*

On Belief in Self:

"Believe deep down in your heart that you're destined to do great things!"

— *Joe Paterno*

71

are self-motivated. They do not wait for someone else to tell them what to do or when to do it. Their interest and desire do not depend on outside circumstances or other people. They possess instead an inner drive for achievement, for action, and for success that keeps them striving for a goal, pushing for advancement, and competing for success.

It seems obvious that if all successful people are self-motivated, possession of this trait is a great advantage. This suggests some questions, such as: *Where does self-motivation originate?* Is it an inborn characteristic or is it a learned skill? Must it be a lifelong attitude or can it be developed at any age?

Over the last few decades, psychologists and behavioral scientists have conducted an enormous body of research in the field of motivation, seeking to learn what motivates people and whether motivation can be increased or intensified. All of the research agrees that the most effective motivation is that which is self-generated and that it is largely a matter of attitude. Since attitudes are merely habits of thought, it follows that self-motivation is a learned skill and that anyone who is willing to invest the time and effort needed to develop a new habit of thought can become self-motivated.

The tool, technique, or procedure that is most effective in developing self-motivation is one with which you are already familiar through lifelong use. It is the tool of affirmation.

On Proving Something:

"Every great champion I've ever met always had something to prove."

— *Bill Glass*

There is power in talking to yourself!

Although this name may be new to you, the process is not. Affirmation may be called self-suggestion, self-talk, self-affirmation, attitude control, or personal reminders. It may simply be called "talking to yourself." We all use affirmation. Its power to control and direct thought has been known for centuries.

The Greek philosopher Plato told his students: *Take charge of your life. You can do what you will with it.*

Buddha taught: *All that we are is the result of what we have thought.*

Marcus Aurelius, the Roman emperor-philosopher, said: *A man's life is what his thoughts make of it.*

Mahatma Gandhi told his followers: *Man often becomes what he believes himself to be. If I keep on saying to myself that I cannot do a certain thing, it is possible that I may end up by really becoming incapable of doing it. On the contrary, if I have the belief that I*

On Self-Praise:

"Self-praise is for losers. Be a winner. Stand for something. Always have class, and be humble."
— *John Madden*

73

can do it, I shall surely acquire the capacity even if I may not have it at the beginning.

William James, the 20th century philosopher, said: *The greatest discovery of my generation is that human beings can alter their lives by altering their attitudes of mind*.

James Allen, in his book, *As a Man Thinketh*, said: *The vision that you glorify, the ideal that you enthrone in your heart — this you will build your life by, this you will become.*

Throughout the centuries, wise men have understood the necessity for building attitudes and belief and confidence in your own capabilities by reminding yourself of what you can be and what you can become. The nature of this dynamic tool is little understood; it is, therefore, greatly neglected. Perhaps it is the very simplicity of affirmation that causes it to be overlooked.

Just what is affirmation? The dictionary calls affirmation the positive assertion of the truth or validity of a statement. Perhaps it would be clearer for our purposes to say that an affirmation is a positive declaration that describes what

On Expectations:

"Failures are expected by losers, ignored by winners."

— *Joe Gibbs*

you want to be, what you want to have, or how you want to live your life.

Because we live in a scientific, industrial society, we tend to demand visible, tangible, concrete evidence, and we tend to discount or reject ideas, concepts, and truths that we cannot immediately see or feel. It is, therefore, difficult for us to grasp the significance of this simple tool — affirmation — in a program of personal growth and development.

For hundreds of years, people have used affirmations and have, in a sense, recognized the power of affirmation to affect attitudes, self-confidence, and behavior patterns. But, it is a fairly modern idea to pursue a deliberate course of repeating specific mottos for the purpose of producing a desired effect.

You have probably heard of Dr. Emile Coué, the French physician of the late 19th century, who told his patients that they would improve faster if they adopted the simple plan of saying over and

> **"Do not let what you cannot do interfere with what you can do."**
> — *John Wooden*

over: Every day, in every way, I'm getting better and better.

Dr. Coué even affirmed that daily use of this statement would result in the curing of physical ailments, as well as in the development of healthier, happier attitudes. A lot of people laughed at Dr. Coué. His method was so simple that they doubted its validity. But those who followed his instruction found that his method worked in spite of the ridicule of

On Work:

"One thing I never want to be accused of is not working."

— *Don Shula*

others. Dr. Coué understood the power of affirmation. He knew that the repetition of a positive thought over and over, day after day, affects the subconscious mind — the creative power within.

We all use various affirmations, whether we realize it or not. Quotations, proverbs, sayings, and axioms are all affirmations.

For example:

- **A penny saved is a penny earned.**

- **A stitch in time saves nine.**

- **A bird in the hand is worth two in the bush.**

All of these are borrowed affirmations — ideas we have appropriated from someone else to support our personal value system.

Affirmations are powerful ... only when used!

Borrowed affirmations are the most commonly used. But they are effective only when they are genuinely internalized so that their borrowed quality is overcome. But we all use other kinds of self-talk in addition to borrowed affirmations. Have you ever said something like this to yourself:

On Whining:

"I can't stand it when a player whines to me or his teammates or his wife or the writers or anyone else. A whiner is almost always wrong. A winner never whines."

— **Paul Brown**

- **I can do better than that, or**

- **I must remember to use that idea, or**

- **I'll put this in a place where I'll be sure to find it.**

The purpose of such self-talk is to create change, to ensure a future action, to correct an error, or to overcome a bad habit.

Although everyone engages in self-talk to one degree or another, we are sometimes slightly embarrassed to admit that we talk to ourselves. You have probably heard it said laughingly that those who talk to themselves are crazy, especially if they talk out loud. If this were true, we would all be forced to admit to some degree of insanity, for everyone does engage in self-talk.

Talking to yourself may be conscious and directed or it may be subliminal and automatic. But you do engage in self-talk, and that, in essence, is what affirmation is. Since you are already practicing self-talk, or affirmation, what could be more simple or practical than to turn the habit to your advantage by giving it your attention, recognizing its importance, and controlling its content?

Affirmation is merely controlled and directed self-talk which gives direction and impact to your plans and goals for self-improvement, and results in greater utilization of your potential for success.

On Publicity:

"Publicity is like poison; it doesn't hurt unless you swallow it."

— *Joe Paterno*

The present pattern of your personality and your life is the result of all the influences to which you have been exposed since your birth, together with your reactions to, and your feelings about, those experiences. Your automatic or unconscious self-talk reflects the feelings and emotions with which you have up to this time reacted to the experiences of the past. They are stored in the memory banks of your computer brain. You can never lose this past programming, but you may add to it. Because new input into your memory has the strength of freshness. It can override negative conditioning. But it is effective only for a short period of time unless it is strengthened and reinforced by repetition. Constant repetition produces acceptance and, finally, belief. The new habits follow.

How affirmations work

When you set a goal and affirm it through self-talk, you exert a psychological reinforcement of your opinions and ideas. You create belief in yourself and your ability to become whatever you wish to be. You may say: *But this does not alter reality. The fact that I believe doesn't change the way things really are.*

Objectively, affirmation does not change anything, but subjectively, it certainly does. You tend to live up to what is expected of you, to your reputation, good or bad. But you not only live up to what others expect of you, you also live

On Your Strong Points:

"Build up your weaknesses until they become your strong points."

— *Knute Rockne*

up to what you expect of yourself. This is why the use of affirmation is such a dynamic tool for personal development. Expectation exerts a powerful force.

The modern novelist, John Steinbeck, observed: *It is the nature of man to rise to greatness, if greatness is expected of him.*

Norman Vincent Peale, the author of *The Power of Positive Thinking*, wrote, *When the mental picture or attitude is strongly enough held, it actually seems to control conditions and circumstances.*

An outstanding young tennis professional was asked by a sports announcer how he managed to serve ace points time after time so consistently. The young man answered, "I guess it's just because people expect me to."

> **"You affect your subconscious mind by verbal repetition."**
> — *W. Clement Stone*

You can picture the effects of affirmation on your attitude if you can visualize a seesaw. One end of the board is loaded with the negative responses and ideas you have built up through a lifetime, while the other is weighted with positive ideas. Since childhood, a great deal of input into your attitudes,

---

On Leading:

"Leadership, like coaching, is fighting for the hearts and souls of men and getting them to believe in you."

— *Eddie Robinson*

however well-intended, has been negative. Many of your feelings and attitudes, therefore, may tend to be negative. They may even be so heavy that they cause the negative end of the seesaw to rest firmly on the ground. But the moment you begin to use positive affirmations, you gradually begin to shift the weight in a positive direction. As the balance shifts, the seesaw gradually changes position until a preponderance of positive feelings and reactions govern your life and the negatives are pushed off into oblivion.

> **"Imagination gives you a destination. The greatest gift a coach can give a player, a teacher can give a student, and a parent can give to their child, is the opportunity to imagine great things. These dreams in childhood pave the way for future successes."**
> — *Mike Krzyzewski*

When you consciously practice the technique of affirmation, the law of displacement also begins to operate in your favor. Picture your mind as a bucket into which the icy water of negative feelings and attitudes has been poured all of your life. You can consciously displace this water that chills all of your desire for growth by the use of affirmations. Each affirmation that you use is like a smooth, warm gravel dropped into the bucket of water — a positive force to replace the cold negatives. A large enough

On Future Performance:

"Regarding performance: Yesterday is a cancelled check, today is cash on the line, and tomorrow is a promissory note."

— *Hank Stram*

number of small stones dropped into a bucket of water eventually replaces almost all of the water. The warm, positive thoughts and ideas you repeatedly drop into your store of thoughts, feelings, and beliefs, will gradually warm your life and replace the old chilling negatives.

Through this process of displacing negative attitudes, you begin to form new positive expectations for yourself, and you also begin to believe that you can live up to those expectations. Because you expect to see positive changes, you begin to act in the positive manner you have affirmed. You literally become a changed personality because you act according to the expectations you set for yourself. Your affirmation becomes a self-fulfilling prophecy.

4 types of affirmations to choose from

There are all kinds of affirmations. Let's look at a few of them:

#1 — A numerical affirmation makes use of some sort of number that has a special meaning for you. It may represent money, a score, or a number of activities. For example, a defensive player might use an affirmation such as "4 up, 4 down." This could be a reminder to hold the opposing team to three plays and a punt. Repeating this affirmation over and over gives focus to the defense and the results are mentally and physically visible.

On Conditioning:

"You have to be willing to out-condition your opponents."

— *Bear Bryant*

#2 — *Pictorial affirmations have a powerful effect to intensify and build desire in your subconscious mind.* If you look often at a picture that represents your goal, you stimulate your imagination to help you create and implement means of transforming the picture into reality. A picture of yourself standing with your team winning the conference trophy, the floor plan of your dream house, or travel folders of the vacation spot you want to visit are all powerful affirmations to help you realize your dreams.

I know of an artist who found a way to use a pictorial affirmation. On the door to her double garage she painted a picture of the backs of the two cars she wanted to have — a Mercedes Benz and a Porsche — as though they were parked inside her garage. Every time she approaches her garage she sees the two beautiful cars that she plans to have.

What happened? You guessed it, the day came when what she painted on her garage door ... was actually parked inside her garage!

#3 — *Verbal affirmations are condensed statements of a desired result or an attitude you wish to possess.* For example:

- **I am a great coach.**

- **I am a builder of men.**

On Losing Graciously:

"Show me a good and gracious loser and I'll show you a failure."

— Knute Rockne

- **I live a balanced life.**

- **I am a Total Person.**

- **Everyday I grow as a coach and as a person.**

- **Every year my team has a greater win percentage.**

- **I am in great physical shape as an example for my team.**

- **I know all the members of the team personally.**

#4 — Actions can become affirmations. The repetition of block or tackle until it is mastered is an affirmation. Repeating a new play is an affirmation. Throwing the ball to a receiver is an affirmation. Snapping the ball, breaking from the huddle, and lining up are all affirmations.

Make it a habit!

Developing the art of self-talk or self-suggestion — the use of affirmation — is a habit just like any other habit. There are affirmations for living, affirmations for work, affirmations for overcoming fear, affirmations for personal development, and affirmations to command the morning so you will get off to the right start.

On Being the Best:

"The only yardstick for success our society has is being a champion. No one remembers anything else."

— *John Madden*

Many people have internalized the truth in an affirmation from Norman Vincent Peale's book, *The Tough-Minded Optimist*: **God made me strong. I see myself as I really am, strong. With God's help, I'm not weak, I'm strong. I have what it takes. Thank you, God, for my strength.**

An affirmation used by former Notre Dame coach Frank Leahy is: **When the going gets tough, the tough get going.**

In fact, Leahy had this affirmation painted in gigantic letters on the locker room wall so his players would see it as the last thing before they ran onto the field.

An affirmation may be used effectively the first thing in the morning to help you control your time and your attitude from the very beginning of the day. If you look out of the window and say, "What a miserable day," your spirits fall into the depths of despair. On the other hand, you can say, "This is the day the Lord has made; I will rejoice and be glad in it."

Then you are ready to begin the day on a solid, positive note; and you are well on the way to success. How you

On Moving On:

"I don't apologize for anything. When I make a mistake, I take the blame and go on from there. I just despise to lose, and that has taken a man of mediocre ability and made a pretty good coach out of him."

— *Woody Hayes*

feel depends on your mental stance. Anchor your mind to abiding values and command the morning by their power.

Affirmations can affect your physical well being as powerfully as they affect your mental attitudes. Some medical researchers say that fully 75 percent of patients who visit doctors suffer from psychosomatic illnesses induced by negative thought and fed into the subconscious by negative affirmations. Affirming health and strength predisposes you to experience physical well being, while looking for symptoms of illness and reinforcing them with fear promises illness.

> **"Football games are won a play at a time."**
> — *David Joseph*

Successful people invariably use positive affirmations to support their attitudes and habits. It doesn't matter if you call them mottos, creeds, or principles for action. It's the repetitive, positive input that you experience through repeating and seeing these statements day after day that produces success attitudes. More than three thousand years ago, the wise King Solomon said, "As a man thinketh in his heart, so is he."

Making your own affirmations

Because affirmations are so powerful in bringing about personality change and success, it is a good idea to see that they are planned and constructed to accomplish the

On Belief:

"Before you can win a game, you have to not lose it."

— *Chuck Noll*

greatest good for you. There are some simple but extremely important guidelines for constructing workable affirmations. Your affirmations provide you with confidence to make any changes in your life that are necessary to attain your goal.

The first step is to determine areas in which you wish to make changes in your behavior. Obviously, if you begin to think about the goals that you wish to achieve in your life, and the attitudes, habits, and personality traits that you want to develop, you will see some areas of your life that must change. Before you can make such changes, you must know exactly what you want to become, what you want to do, and what you want to have.

It is most important that you state specifically what you want. A generalization such as "I want to be a better person" is meaningless unless you know exactly what you mean by "better."

If you say, "I want to make more money," but do not define exactly what you mean by "more money," it will be impossible to achieve your goal. For no matter how much you make, you will never feel successful because your affirmation says you must have more money.

If you say, "I want the running team to make more yards per play," you need to define "more yards." Set a specific goal. This does not mean that you put a limit on what

On Creating Atmosphere:

"I don't know what motivation really means but somebody told me one time that motivation is creating an atmosphere in which motivation can take place. And until we do that, then we can't motivate."

— *Erk Russell*

you can do, for when you reach your first goal for increased yardage, you can set a new goal for another increase.

So describe your desire or your goal in specific terms. For example:

- **I want the running team to make 20 percent more yards per play.**

- **I want the team to have 25% less penalties.**

- **I want to delegate more so I have 2 hours per day to be available in the office to speak with players.**

- **I want to host a party at my house this Christmas for the team and their families.**

It is important that you take time to write out a description of the changes in personality, attitudes, and habits that you wish to achieve. Our memories are tricky things. We tend to forget good intentions that call for effort, particularly if they also involve change.

Once you know what goals you want to achieve, you are ready to begin the actual formation of some affirmations you can use to support the changes in your personality, attitudes, or possessions that you have listed as desirable. If your affirmations are to exert a positive impact on your attitudes, they must be constructed according to these basic guidelines:

On Hungry Players:

"The country is full of good coaches. What it takes to win is a bunch of interested players."
— *Don Coryell*

#1 — Use the first person pronoun "I." Because you are an individual, unique in every respect, your affirmations must be uniquely yours. They must be restricted to what "I" can do or become. While you and your spouse, your children, your staff, or your players might use affirmations worded identically, each person must internalize them individually. You are an individual; you will have some differing emotions, feelings, and attitudes toward any situation. Your affirmation, then, should use "I" not "we."

For example, instead of: *We spend money according to our financial plan*, let your affirmation say: ***I spend money in accordance with my family's spending plan***. Instead of: *We plan each day's work activities*, let your affirmation say, ***I plan each day's work and follow my plan***.

#2 — State affirmations positively. There are a number of reasons why affirmations must be stated positively. Much of your early conditioning was loaded with negatives. You were told:

- **Don't run in the street.**

- **Don't play with matches.**

- **Don't bite off more than you can chew.**

- **Don't count your chickens before they hatch.**

On Complaining:

"The man who complains about the way the ball bounces is likely the one who dropped it."
— *Lou Holtz*

Now you are trying to achieve a balance and, eventually, to tip the scales in favor of positives. Negative input, in whatever form, is limiting and self-defeating. You need positive statements to produce positive pictures in your mind. For example, if you use an affirmation such as: *I am not afraid to speak in public*, you have no way to visualize your goal, to experience in your imagination how it would feel to achieve your desire. There are many feelings that are "not fear." Which one is appropriate? You have created a vacuum. There is no motivation, no feeling of urgency, no accomplishment to experience in advance.

In contrast, you can affirm: ***I enjoy the excitement of acceptance and sense of accomplishment I feel when I speak in public***.

Then you can mentally see yourself performing and feeling what you affirm. You actually experience in advance the benefits of reaching your goal to speak effectively. Your affirmation serves as the tipping of the scales, the swing of the pendulum, the balance of the seesaw, away from the negative feelings of fear and failure, toward the positive enjoyment of self-confidence and success.

#3 — State affirmations in the present tense. The suggestion that affirmations be phrased in the present tense probably causes more problems than all other guidelines combined. You may have a mental block against writing or repeating an affirmation when you "know it isn't true."

° On Luck:

"Sure, luck means a lot in football. Not having a good quarterback is bad luck."

— *Don Shula*

89

Remember, an affirmation is merely a tool to achieve the goal of behavior modification. A mechanic uses a wrench to tighten a bolt. The wrench is a tool. It is neither true nor false. So it is with an affirmation. It is a tool used to accomplish a purpose. It is neither true nor false.

Before you can become a different person, before you can be what you wish, before you can have what you want, you must see yourself in your new role and know how it feels to be what you have decided to become, to do what you have decided to do, or to have what you have decided to want.

> **"It's hard to beat a person who never gives up."**
> — *Babe Ruth*

Your present tense affirmation is the tool that lets you experience how these new conditions feel.

If you repeat an affirmation such as, I will save ten percent of my money, you feel no urgency to act on the principle today. However, if you affirm, I save ten percent of my income, you begin immediately to live by your decision to save.

If you say, I will become the head coach, this picture remains always in the future. However, if you affirm daily, *I am head coach*, you begin to form the attitudes, the habits, and the behavior that will prepare you for the day when your affirmation becomes reality. You will know how it feels to be head coach. You will know how you should act and how you

On Eliminating Mistakes:

"Eliminate the mistakes and you'll never lose a game. To eliminate mistakes, you have to pick the right quarterback."

— *Woody Hayes*

should react. When you reach your goal, you will be able to perform effectively because of your affirmations.

#4 — Affirmations must be fun. If you make a drudgery of the process of writing and using affirmations, you reinforce existing negative attitudes. The requirement for enjoying affirmations involves the full stretch of your imagination to visualize the future. It goes hand-in-hand with the concept that motivation arises from anticipation of the fulfillment of needs and desires.

#5 — Affirmations must be written. Writing crystallizes thought, and thought motivates action. Writing keeps you on track. Writing is a reminder that wards off distraction. Writing helps you visualize results.

Your unconscious mind — which does not distinguish between fact and fancy — accepts the image you have constructed while writing and reviewing your affirmations. Then gradually your behavior responds, and you become the person you have affirmed yourself to be.

Repeat daily

All of the inspiring and motivational affirmations you write must be used repeatedly to produce effective results. Part of the purpose behind writing is the provision of the

On Confidence:

"You need to play with supreme confidence, or else you'll lose again, and then losing becomes a habit."

— *Joe Paterno*

means to use your affirmations with spaced repetition. This point cannot be overemphasized.

Remember, you got where you are today through the influence of spaced repetition. You can change habits, attitudes, and personality characteristics in the same way through controlled repetition. Written affirmations may be used in dozens of ways to reinforce the habits and attitudes you wish to develop. One of the simplest devices is to write them on small cards and carry them in your wallet or pocket calendar. Keep them in your desk drawer or somewhere else where you will see them several times a day. Read them over and over.

> **"Man's mind, stretched to a new idea, never goes back to its original dimensions."**
> — *Oliver Wendell Holmes*

There are many ways to use the affirmations that you are willing for others to see. You can tape them to the bathroom or bedroom mirror, to the refrigerator door, to the locker door, or to the sun visor of your car. You can tack them on a bulletin board at the office or at home.

Keep a copy of your affirmations on your bedside table and read them as soon as you wake in the morning, and the last thing before you turn out the lights at night. Beginning the day with positive expectancy provides you with a head start for achievement. Ending the day with positive affirmation prepares you for rest and relaxation that will bring you renewal for success tomorrow.

On Growing:

"Don't ever stop learning; you never know it all."
— *Don Faurot*

On the other hand, many affirmations are personal. Remember this as you plan how to use them. Because your affirmations are tied to personal goals, it is often difficult for anyone else to see the reason behind them. If you share your private affirmations with people who do not understand the purpose and the operation of affirmation as a tool, you invite negative input from people who see you as you are now — not as you have decided to be. They do not know what goals you have chosen to achieve. Their negative input might slow down the benefits you can gain from using affirmations.

Try to fit the planned use for each affirmation to its subject matter. For example, a financial affirmation can be placed in your wallet or checkbook where you will see it each time you think about money. A time-organization affirmation may be placed in your pocket appointment book, or at the head of your "Daily Do" list. An affirmation about eating habits may be placed on the refrigerator door or the bathroom scales. Exercise your imagination and your creativity to devise unique ways of using your affirmations for fun. You should enjoy becoming the person you want to be. Life is meant to be savored. Achievement loses its meaning if you fail to enjoy the process.

When you begin to use affirmations, you release the full potential of your creative power. You find yourself developing new ways of doing things and of achieving goals. Here

On Belief:

"Don't tell your problems to people: eighty percent don't care; and the other twenty percent are glad you have them."

— *Lou Holtz*

are some examples of positive affirmations that suggest action and results:

- I always plan my work.

- I organize my efforts today for tomorrow and the future.

- I plan ahead to get ahead.

- I have complete confidence in all that I think and do.

- I treat a problem as an opportunity for creativity; as a result, my life is enriched.

- I persevere and finish any task I undertake.

- I bring great concentration to bear upon the subject at hand.

- I courageously face all problems and solve them easily.

- I have the ability to reach creative decisions.

On Making the Team Work:

"Individual commitment to a group effort — that is what makes a team work, a company work, a society work, a civilization work."

— *Vince Lombardi*

Plan to use affirmation in every area of your life. In the mental area, you might affirm:

- **I am intelligent.**

- **I can understand and apply new ideas creatively.**

- **I eagerly receive new ideas and use the ones that apply to my needs.**

In the social realm, you might use affirmations like these:

- **I love other people and find it easy to express my interest and concern.**

- **I express my interest in others by listening creatively to their ideas.**

- **I enjoy getting to know my players and my staff.**

In the family area, affirmations such as these might work for you:

On Quitting:

"Never quit. It is the easiest cop-out in the world. Set a goal and don't quit until you attain it. When you do attain it, set another goal, and don't quit you reach it. Never quit."

— **Bear Bryant**

- **I provide a regular time for sharing and communicating with each member of my family.**

- **I enjoy recreation and family activities with my spouse and children.**

- **I provide the emotional and psychological support that my family needs from me.**

- **I relate to members of my family in a positive way.**

Affirmations are important in the physical area. You might use some affirmations like these:

- **I maintain excellent physical fitness through my personal program of exercise, good diet, and adequate rest and recreation.**

- **I maintain a regular schedule of physical activity.**

- **I handle the stresses of everyday life with calmness and serenity.**

Use your imagination, your creativity, and your initiative in planning and using affirmation as a tool to develop self-motivation. Your life will be filled with heightened excitement and eager anticipation of each day.

On Losing:

"Losing is easy. It's not enjoyable, but it's easy."
— *Bud Wilkinson*

2 final reminders

As you prepare to reach your next set of goals, here are two final reminders:

First, affirmations never substitute for action. There is no magical power connected with the repetition of a statement, other than the dynamic effect it has on your belief in yourself. You cannot say to yourself every morning and every night, "I am a millionaire," then sit down and do nothing, expecting a million dollars to fall into your lap.

If, on the other hand, you constantly affirm, "I am a millionaire," and begin to think and act the part by becoming more productive in your work, by managing your money properly and by investing your savings wisely, the possibility of becoming a millionaire increases daily. Your affirmation becomes a self-fulfilling prophecy, not because of some magical quality, but because of your own actions.

Second, affirmations require patience. You must be patient when you first begin to use affirmations. If you expect instantaneous dramatic results, you will become tense and actually slow down the effect that an affirmation could produce. Remember, it took many years for you to become the person you are. Change requires time.

On History:

"Ask people over the last 20 years who has won the most Commander-in-Chief's Trophies. Tradition always is under construction. People don't look at what happened in the 1940s. They look at what's happening today."

— *Lou Holtz*

The present and the future are not joined by a single link, but by a chain composed of the goals you have set, the plans you have made to achieve them, and the affirmations that you repeat to displace negative thoughts, and the actions you take.

> **"You only live once, but if you work it right, once is enough."**
> — *Joe E. Lewis*

There is no escaping it, we all talk to ourselves, whether consciously or unconsciously. Sure, it's an awesome power, so why not put it to work for your own benefit!

On Sacrifice:

"A man can be as great as he wants to be. If you believe in yourself and have the courage, the determination, the dedication, the competitive drive and if you are willing to sacrifice the little things in life and pay the price for the things that are worthwhile, it can be done."

— *Vince Lombardi*

On How You See Yourself:

"Be positive about yourself."

— *Mack Brown*

Chapter 6
STEP #3 — Create Passion & Desire

On Passion:

"It is better to have died as a small boy than to fumble this football."

— *John Heisman*

STEP #3
Create Passion & Desire

Clearly defined goals have a way of creating such passion and desire in you to succeed that nothing can stand in your way. You are sure of your course, you are enthusiastic, and you are self-motivated to do whatever it takes to accomplish your goal.

The truth is, passion and desire are essential elements for every individual, and especially so since you are a coach.

Passion and desire open doors

As you know, talent creates its own opportunities, but where does talent come from? It comes from passion and desire. They are the catalysts and developers of talent. They combine to create their own opportunities and abilities. They open doors that previously were closed ... or didn't even exist!

On Mental Preparation:

"There is no question that the best motivation is to be prepared mentally, to know what you are going to do when you go out to play."
— *Vince Dooley*

Every advance in history has resulted from one person's desire to change the status quo, to win a race with time, with customs, traditions, or with self. This is why passion and desire burn like a flame in the heart of every achiever.

The difference between winning and losing *is decided by passion and desire!* When you see people who are full of passion and desire, they no doubt:

- **Keep working** to solve problems when others have already given up.

- **Make commitments** while other people make half-hearted promises.

- **Have the courage** to stand up for their actions, while others remain unsure and tentative.

- **Seem restless and aggressive** to some degree, while others settle into apathy and complacency.

- **Take personal responsibility** for more than themselves, while others either say, "It's not my fault," or ask, "What's in it for me?"

- **Are committed** to the goal before them, while others daydream or make half-hearted attempts to accomplish something.

On Leading Others:

"I don't know of any other way to lead but by example."

— *Don Shula*

- **Respect everyone** around them.

- **Possess an insatiable appetite** for creative thinking, for action, and for achievement, while others accept the status quo.

- **Push themselves** to work harder, while others make excuses and slow down.

- **Remain thirsty** for greater success, while others are satisfied when they happen to accomplish a goal.

You, no doubt, possess these qualities, but if you want to increase your passion and desire, it can be done.

5 steps to developing passion and desire

Passion and desire are developed as the result of being challenged. How you choose to react to a challenge determines your destiny. It also determines how fast you will allow passion and desire to grow inside of you!

Here are the five steps to developing passion and desire:

#1) GAIN SELF-KNOWLEDGE: Learn what excites and energizes you. Know what motivates you to take action. Crystallize your thinking and your objectives and clarify your

On Giving Loyalty:

"If you're going to expect loyalty, give loyalty. That's not a one-way ticket."

— *Darrell Royal*

own personal sense of values so that you know exactly what you believe about yourself, about life in general, and about other people. Only with adequate self-knowledge can you identify the goals that will produce enough challenge and interest to create the passion and desire you must have if you are to achieve them.

#2) MAKE YOUR GOALS MEANINGFUL TO YOU: Too often, the goals we are told to achieve are someone else's goals, and as a result, we are not internally motivated to achieve them. People reach for the minimum, the standard, and the average rather than aspiring to reach the maximum heights to which they are capable.

> **"Passion can be transmitted to others, while desire can be learned and developed as a habit."**
> — *Paul J. Meyer*

#3) LEARN FROM THOSE AROUND YOU: Work to find wisdom and knowledge in those who are in a position to advise you. Respect their insight, expertise, and superior years of experience. Ponder the advice they offer, but always remember that it is your responsibility alone to make the decisions that determine the destiny of you and your team. As much as others may care for you and wish the best for you, no one else is capable of seeing into your inner-most heart to understand your deepest needs and desires.

On Motivation:

"The closer you get to that kid, the more you know him, the more you are going to get out of him, and the more success he's going to have."
— *John Cooper*

#4) VISUALIZE YOUR OWN SUCCESS: There is nothing that increases your passion and desire for achievement like controlled and directed visualization. Something unique and amazing happens when you practice looking into the future to see yourself in possession of your goals. You become so excited, so motivated, and so passionate to reach them that nothing can deter you or draw you off course.

#5) WORK HARDER THAN EVER BEFORE: Be willing to work harder and longer without complaining. No goal exerts enough power to produce passion and desire unless you are willing to invest much of your time and effort in bringing it to fruition. When you have invested a part of yourself in the achievement of some worthy purpose, your passion and desire know no bounds.

How to ignite passion and desire in others

Most likely, you are overflowing with passion and desire. That's the way coaches are, but how can you ignite the same passion and desire in those on your team?

Obviously, making everyone complete the five steps above is the answer, but you cannot force anyone to have passion and desire. It doesn't work that way. You choose to have passion and desire, and so must those on your team. It's a personal choice.

On Wanting to Win:

"There are two things that really motivate — the pull of desire and the push of discontent. You have to want to win and you have to have something you are trying to prove."

— Bill Glass

Of course, there are things you as a coach can do to help them choose passion and desire.

#1) START WITH YOUR ASSISTANT COACHES: Who are the assistant leaders on your team? Begin with them. Explain how you are developing passion and desire in your own life by applying the five steps above. Leaders will step forward and take action. They, like you, will do what it takes to develop passion and desire in their own lives.

> **"You've got to have a dream and you can accomplish unbelievable things if you really believe in it enough."**
> **— Bob Richardson**

#2) SHARE YOUR PLAN WITH THE WHOLE TEAM: Tell everyone on your team what you are doing and how to do it. Whether it is a team meeting, e-mail, or a face-to-face talk with each team player, it is important that everyone be on the same page and that they have the "how to" in hand. They need to be involved in the process.

#3) EXPLAIN WHAT YOU WANT: You are looking for passion and desire because of the lasting benefits that come as a result. A pep rally is not what you want, as the end result leaves no lasting benefit with you or the team.

#4) LEAD BY EXAMPLE: When you work to build your passion and desire, others will follow. They are watching to

On Desire:

"Guts win more games than ability."
— **Bob Zuppke**

see if you will spend the time and energy it takes to develop passion and desire.

#5) PUSH THEM IN: Nobody learns to swim by sitting on the edge of the pool. Get people involved. Push them into the water, even if the task looks difficult. When people are working, passion and desire follow swiftly. Of course, you won't let them drown, but they must be in the water and involved. That is how they will learn the fastest!

#6) CONTINUALLY GUIDE THEM: Always point them back to positive personal development and how to develop passion and desire. If they have questions, show them how to find the answers. If they complain, help them find a solution. If they worry, help them take control. If they don't think they can do it, help them take the first step.

#7) BE WILLING TO MAKE MISTAKES: We all make mistakes. That is just the way it is, but those who are so afraid of making mistakes will seldom do anything. If you make it known that mistakes are okay, that taking risks is a

On Motivation:

"When you talk about motivation, your job is to teach attitude and that attitude is an everyday experience. It is easy to tell when a kid is not performing well or having trouble on the campus with teachers and grades — then you know immediately that you have to take the steps to correct that. I think that, more than anything else, is important to motivation."

— Bo Schembechler

good thing, it will free people to move forward. You can always fix the mistake later. Winning *and* losing moves you closer toward your goal ... and the team is developing passion and desire!

#8) PROVIDE THE RIGHT ENVIRONMENT: To be effective, you must provide the right conditions, opportunities, and environment for those you lead ... so they can develop self-motivation. Your ability to inspire self-motivation will ignite passion and desire like nothing else will!

Measuring passion and desire

How do you tell the difference between serious passion and senseless zeal or between focused desire and clueless ambition? A lot of people want things desperately, but they don't have the passion and desire necessary. They have dreams but no real goals.

As a coach, you need to discern when people have what it takes ... and when they don't. You can determine that by asking those on your team these questions:

- **What are the obstacles or roadblocks you must overcome to reach the overall goals you desire?**

- **What must you give in time and effort to overcome those obstacles and obtain what you desire?**

On Motivation:

"I believe that knowledge and preparation are the keys to motivation."

— *Tom Landry*

- **What are the rewards you will experience when you have succeeded?**

- **Are the rewards worth what it will cost you in time and effort?**

If players can answer these questions with clear answers, then you can bet that passion and desire are genuine!

When you and those on your team are armed with passion and desire, you literally become success magnets. The law of attraction is free to work for you. You begin to attract whatever it is you need to be successful. Your enthusiasm electrifies everyone who comes in contact with you. Passion and desire combine to give you the extra energy and the extra determination to reach out for whomever and whatever you need to accomplish the job.

> **"Most football players are temperamental. That is 90 percent temper and 10 percent mental."**
> — *Doug Plank*

When you catch a vision of greatness and crystallize your thinking about the goals you want to pursue, passion and desire flare into a powerful flame that warms, energizes, and empowers you!

On a Greater Cause:

"We teach our players the need, that there is a need and we stress the need that they are going to participate in a winning activity. Then, they have a desire to really contribute and then they perceive their cause to be great."

— *Bear Bryant*

109

Passion and desire required

Vibrant, successful teams *require* passionate, desire-driven coaches. The entire organization creates an internal passion and desire for success by striving for a vision, mission, and purpose larger than itself.

As you lead by example, your team rises to the occasion as well ... and they demand more from you! This in turn creates even greater momentum as you and your team move forward.

Passion and desire can only be satisfied with greater success and more passion and desire. This is a combustive cycle of growth that everyone wants to be a part of!

On Life or Death:

"When you are playing for the national championship, it's not a matter of life or death. It's more important than that."

— *Duffy Daugherty*

On Winning:

"How you respond to the challenge in the second half will determine what you become after the game, whether you are a winner or a loser."
— *Lou Holtz*

Chapter 7
STEP #4 — Develop Confidence & Trust

On Confidence:

"Confidence is contagious. So is lack of confidence."

— *Vince Lombardi*

STEP #4
Develop Confidence & Trust

Y ou are where you are and who you are because of the dominating thoughts that occupy your mind — *no more and no less*. Confidence and trust in your own ability to innovate, develop, persevere, and succeed are key ingredients in your current and future success.

But no matter how much confidence and trust you have in yourself, when it comes to leading others, they must have confidence and trust in you.

What's more, there is confidence and trust that need to be developed within the team.

The challenge is to create an atmosphere where people have confidence and trust 1) in you, 2) in themselves, and 3) in the team as a whole.

As the coach, that challenge is your job.

On Communication:

"You have to be able to communicate with all types of players, and if you care and are concerned, they'll recognize that. Communication will be two ways, and you will get their support if you have that trust."

— *Frank Broyles*

#1: Confidence and trust in you

What can you do to cause others to put their confidence and trust in you? The absolute best way is to lead by example, by having great confidence and trust in yourself and by doing what is right for the team.

Since you are a coach, I assume that leading by example comes naturally to you. You already have great confidence and trust in yourself and you do what is right for your team. Sure, you might make mistakes, but you are quick to take responsibility and find new ways to reach your goals.

Based on that, you are able to help those on your team build confidence and trust in themselves.

#2: Confidence and trust in themselves

Helping those on your team gain confidence and trust in themselves begins by you showing confidence and trust in them. Like you, they aren't perfect, but you are willing to extend yourself, to believe in them, and to empower them, so that their confidence and trust in themselves can increase.

Begin by delegating as much as you can. Inspect what you expect, but always work to build up the people to whom you delegate. Your goal is to work yourself out of a job, sometimes literally, but the self-confidence and trust that comes from this in incredible!

On Treating Others:

"I think in my own mind, it's extremely important to really like people, just to truly, genuinely like and love your players."

— *Don Coryell*

The act of delegating not only benefits those on your team, but it also enables you to multiply your efforts. But, unfortunately, delegating is often misunderstood.

Your job as the coach is to control the **results of what is delegated**, not the team member. By having confidence and trust in other people, and then helping them accomplish a given task correctly, you are helping people develop confidence and trust in themselves. They have more confidence and trust in you as well.

> **"To be trusted is a greater compliment than to be loved."**
> — *George MacDonald*

Delegating is truly a win-win situation for everyone.

Make every effort to empower others. As you show confidence and trust in others, you are empowering them. You are helping them grow. As a result, they become more capable individuals, taking more personal responsibility and needing less monitoring. In short, they are becoming leaders!

Be part of the team. Being part of a team means thinking, talking, and acting as a team. Seeing yourself as part of the team, even though you are the coach, will affect what you say. Words like "me" should be exchanged for "we," and "I" should be exchanged for "us." Team players can tell if you are truly part of the team by what you say.

On Teamwork:

"An excellent team is a group of people who play better than their parts."

— *John Madden*

You must also consider your actions. When you think and talk like a team player, then your actions will line up with that. It's all part of being a team.

Be available. Being available does not mean that you end up doing all the work. Rather, it means that the capable people on your team can get your assistance if they need it. They know you have not abandoned them, that you are accessible, while at the same time you are not micro-managing them.

Work to develop potential. Those on your team have unlimited potential, just like you do. *As the coach, you are in a unique position because you can see the potential in people often before they do.* Through your confidence and trust in them, you can relay that information to them, helping them reach more of their potential.

Show them how to change their attitudes. Those on your team who are serious about bettering themselves will eventually need to address their attitudes. Attitudes are difficult to change because they are based on personal values. What we value determines what we pay attention to and it dictates our habits of thought, and determines our attitudes.

It is difficult, if not impossible, to change attitudes without first restructuring the values that are the essential

On Confidence:

"Leadership is a matter of having people look at you and gain confidence, seeing how you react. If you're in control, they're in control."

— *Tom Landry*

building blocks of those new attitudes. Values, which have been established since birth, are deeply rooted and can only be removed when "traded" for another value. This trading process requires that you dig to the bottom of an issue and in the end, you make a personal choice to change.

That is why attitudes are so hard to change. There are no quick fixes. The good news is that when people choose to change, their attitudes follow suit. Helping people reach their full potential will inevitably affect their values, which in turn affects their attitudes. It is a process that works every time.

Focus on personal development. Regardless of your personal goals or the team's goals, it is important that you always focus on the personal development of each team member. A certain goal in one area of a team member's life is very important to that person, so do what you can to help that goal become a reality. It shows that you really care and that the goal is worth pursuing.

Urgency can keep you focused on immediate needs and pressing issues, but the big picture is personal development. Neither you nor your team can afford to lose sight of that!

> "When someone believes in you, it raises your confidence level and allows you to try things that are impossible to do by yourself."
> — *Mike Krzyzewski*

Keep your eye on the bottom line. One law of physics states that a body at rest tends to stay at rest. As a

On Success:

"Success is not forever and failure isn't fatal."
— *Don Shula*

117

coach, you will see people at rest ... tending to stay at rest. You must help them get up, take action, and get results.

This does not mean that results are more important than people. Rather, it's just a statement about people's natural tendency to stay at rest. They need a good push in the right direction, with kindness!

You know that nothing happens until someone takes action. By helping people take action, you are training them to keep their mind in the game and their eye on the prize.

#3: Confidence and trust in the team

When a team has confidence and trust in itself, that is a powerful sign of just how far the team has come. Naturally, it takes time and positive experiences to increase the team's confidence and trust, but there are some things you can do to expedite that process.

Always look for the positive. You will always find what you are looking for ... and this principle is especially true of your team. If, as a team, you are looking for opportunities and are willing and able to creatively address whatever comes your way, you will find new ways to accomplish any goal. Obstacles that seem insurmountable to others can be overcome by the team.

Unfortunately, those who look for reasons why a goal cannot be achieved will find plenty of reasons why defeat and failure should be accepted. Nobody wants to be part of a

On Believing the Best:

"Always talk positive with what you've got."
— *Mack Brown*

118

failing team, which is why negative-minded teams fall apart very quickly. People thrive in a positive atmosphere, but shrivel up in a negative one.

Believe in the team's unlimited potential. Just as an *individual* has unlimited potential, so does a *team* have unlimited potential. However, believing in that potential is the first necessary step.

When it is your habit to think of your team as having unlimited potential, you have the building block for a highly effective team.

Focusing on unlimited potential allows room for personal growth by everyone on your team as well as team growth as as whole.

> "Trust men and they will be true to you. Trust them greatly and they will show them-selves great."
> — Ralph Waldo Emerson

Build the individual. Just as you have personal goals, so does everyone else on your team. By actively working with individuals to help them reach their personal goals, you are increasing the confidence and trust in the team.

When it comes to goals, assistants and players usually face two options: the team's goals or their own personal goals. It's an either-or decision.

On Staying Focused:

"Don't give up at halftime. Concentrate on winning the second half."
— *Bear Bryant*

But when you help people reach their personal goals while the team also reaches its goals, people love it! They are sold on being part of the team and part of you!

Confidence and trust take time

It takes time for people to put their confidence and trust in you, in themselves, and in the team. It's not a rapid process. In the instant-gratification, quick-fix world of today, it would be nice if you could just push the "fast forward" button so that everybody would have the confidence and trust they need, but it doesn't work that way.

The time spent in building confidence and trust is necessary, good, and beneficial.

Building confidence and trust will do more for you and for your team than you could ever imagine!

On Treating Players:

"Treat all of your players as individuals, as men. You give them responsibility. You give them pride."

— *Frank Broyles*

On Preparation:

"I don't believe in team motivation. I believe in getting a team prepared so it knows it will have the necessary confidence when it steps on a field and be prepared to play a good game."

— *Tom Landry*

Chapter 8
STEP #5 — Foster Commitment & Responsibility

On Perseverance:

"A winner never stops trying."

— *Tom Landry*

STEP #5
Foster Commitment & Responsibility

Quitting is the No.1 reason why people fail to reach a goal. In fact, 90% of all failure comes from quitting. The answer, then, is simply not to quit!

What is interesting is that the people who do give up and quit are usually just as capable of succeeding as you or anyone else. They have the potential and the ability, yet they choose to quit.

What could they have done differently? Did they lack a necessary ingredient for success? *Whatever the situation and whatever the question, remove the 90% chance of failure by simply refusing to quit!*

You can do that by fostering commitment and responsibility among those on your team.

On Loyalty:

"Loyalty is a two-way street. The leader must exhibit loyalty to those in the organization. A sincere belief in your staff and how they're doing their jobs can get tested during a bad season."

— *Grant Teaff*

The 5 elements of commitment

Commitment is the difference between winning and losing, between success and failure. Commitment is comprised of five key elements:

ELEMENT #1: Raw determination. This is the refusal to give up, to quit, or to be defeated. Determination is a result of the confidence created by written and specific goals. Individuals who lack a detailed understanding of where they want to go and why they want to go there will never feel secure about their goals.

> **"You alone are responsible for what you can become."**
> — *Paul J. Meyer*

Because they have failed to fully crystallize their thinking, they never really know whether the goals they've chosen are correct! Armed with a clear, concise plan of action, you and your team feel secure enough to push ahead. They know that their efforts will pay off handsomely in the end.

ELEMENT #2: Patience. Are they willing to keep at a job, task, or goal despite temporary setbacks and encroaching difficulties? Are they willing to work hard now in exchange for a future reward?

ELEMENT #3: A sense of pride. You can be proud if you are using your full potential for success. Of course, this

On Everyone Playing a Part:

"I try to make every player on my team feel he's the spark keeping our machine in motion."
— *Knute Rockne*

kind of pride is unrelated to the boastful arrogance displayed by those who substitute words for actions.

For you and your team, pride in winning is evidenced by the quiet, internal satisfaction of knowing that each of you has contributed the best effort possible and that the resulting achievement is significant and worthwhile.

ELEMENT #4: The ability to take risks. You may be willing to take appropriate risks to ensure the achievement of a goal, but are those on your team willing to do the same?

Of course, nobody can predict the end result of every endeavor, but you want people on your team who are at least willing to step into the unknown by taking a risk. They are willing to attempt a new thing, believing that they can do it.

ELEMENT #5: Knowledge that adversity is good. Most people see a challenge coming and immediately run away. The faster they can run in the opposite direction from adversity the better.

But people who understand commitment know that adversity is a good thing. In fact, they are thankful for adversity because they have learned that in every adversity is the seed of a greater or at least equivalent benefit.

When you face adversity, you are literally forced to use more of your full potential for achievement. Adversity, difficulty, and temporary defeat are stepping stones in disguise — stepping stones to greater success and achievement.

On Taking Responsibility:

"Life is ten percent what happens to you and ninety percent how you respond to it."

— *Lou Holtz*

The 4 elements of responsibility

Taking responsibility is a trademark of every success-ful person alive! There are no exceptions. Those who succeed are people who have learned to take responsibility.

The four elements of responsibility include:

ELEMENT #1: **Knowing the buck stops here.** President Harry Truman had a plaque on his desk that read: "The Buck Stops Here!" He understood that he carried the weight of important decisions. Today, virtually every coach shoulders some element of responsibility for outcomes. The burden you bear may not be as great as Truman's, but the same sentiment still applies. As a coach, you are the respon-sible party.

Accept the fact that nothing — *absolutely nothing* — you do in your organization will produce the successful results you desire until you choose to accept personal respon-sibility for what happens to you and your team.

ELEMENT #2: **Never blaming others.** People cry "victim" all the time, blaming others for their situation, even when it's obvious that they created the entire problem them-selves.

But those who accept responsibility know that blam-ing others is a worthless expenditure of energy and effort. Blaming people leaves us with less energy for growth, improvement, and success. Great coaches don't blame others,

On Team Reality:

"People are needed, but nobody is necessary."
— *Paul Brown*

relive past failures, or repeat mistakes over and over again. They let it go, learn from it, and then move on.

ELEMENT #3: **Making it personal.** People who take responsibility recognize they are responsible for not only who they are and how they feel, but they also are responsible for their own actions. They make it personal.

For example, they don't quit for the day just because they have fulfilled the minimum daily requirements for keeping the doors open. They go the extra mile to keep their commitments to everyone they work with, and they do this even when nobody else is watching. As a result, they exceed everyone's expectations ... regularly!

ELEMENT #4: **Being willing to change.** Personal and professional growth is always a choice. People cannot be forced to become more than they are, but those who accept responsibility are quick to change.

What's more, they are willing to pay the price and accept the responsibility for personal growth. As a result they are the first to grow,

> "There are only two options regarding commitment. You're either IN or you're OUT. There's no such thing as life in-between."
> — *Pat Riley*

to excel, and to increase. When opportunity arises, they are the first to take advantage of it because they are ready.

On Focus:

"I've learned that something constructive comes from every defeat."
— *Tom Landry*

The 5 signs of commitment & responsibility

What sets those who choose to be committed and accept responsibility apart? Are there signs that make it clear just who is committed, who accepts responsibility, and who doesn't? You bet ... and it shows in the bottom line.

Here are the top five signs:

SIGN #1: **Always focused.** Those who are committed and take responsibility are always focused. They cannot be knocked off track, they keep the goal in mind no matter what others say, and they leave no room for discouragement despite popular opinion.

When faced with roadblocks and obstacles, the committed and responsible declare, "I'm going around, through, or over this!" Then they set out to make it happen.

> **"We must either find a way, or make one."**
> **— Hannibal**

SIGN #2: **Able to dream.** Being able to dream is a sign that people are committed and willing to take responsibility. They know how to dream and how to use their imagination to creatively find solutions and ways to reach their goals.

Most of us have negative past experiences that attempt to destroy our creative thinking. Teachers and parents may have even told us to "quit daydreaming and get to work." The

On Taking Chances:

"Do you want to be safe and good, or do you want to take a chance and be great?"
— Jimmy Johnson

natural inference is that any attempt to crystallize or visualize the future is somehow a wasted effort.

The sad consequence is that a lot of people have lost their ability to dream, but those who are committed and take responsibility have overcome these roadblocks. They know how to dream and they combine dreaming with hard work to reach their goals.

SIGN #3: **Always be 100% real.** Those who are committed and accept responsibility are real. They acknowledge their own weaknesses, draw on their own strengths, and analyze where they stand now in relation to where they want to go.

> "The price of greatness is responsibility."
> — *Winston S. Churchill*

When you are real, you don't cover things up. It is tempting to deny that personality characteristics or personal traits even exist, but this leads to complacency. When you courageously and objectively face yourself and your situation, you are able to paint a realistic picture of what needs to be done to reach a given goal.

Those who are 100% real also know that past performance is not a reflection of future potential. They do not take it personally, letting it affect their inner worth as a human. They admit mistakes, learn, and then move on.

On Commitment:

"Coaching is an everyday event. It is not something we do just on practice days or game days or in season. It is something that you do all year."

— *Bo Schembechler*

SIGN #4: **Ready to start.** Without question, those who are committed and take responsibility are the first to start. In fact, they are always ready to go. Having people on your team who are ready — day in and day out — to do whatever it takes to win, is a sure sign of commitment and responsibility.

SIGN #5: **Able to make choices.** Those who are committed and take responsibility are also able to make choices, even when the choices aren't pleasant. They do not retreat in fear. Instead, they push forward with courage, conviction, and determination.

The results of commitment & responsibility

What are the results of continued commitment and responsibility? In a nutshell: everything good!

> "The test of success is not what you do when you're on top. Success is how high you bounce when you hit the bottom."
> — *General George Patton*

To begin with, the fact that 90% of all failure comes from quitting does not apply. Nobody on your team is quitting, so the 90% statistic is irrelevant.

What's more, you and everyone on your team, are open, willing, and doing whatever it takes to reach your full potential. This means that you are able to reach goals even beyond what you've imagined to date!

On Cheating:

"If you cheat to win, you've lost. That's all there is to it."

— *Paul Dietzel*

Fostering commitment and responsibility in yourself and among those on your team is not only a sign that you are an incredible coach, but also you and your team are on your way to unlimited success!

On Taking Responsibility:

"The superior man blames himself. The inferior man blames others."

— *Don Shula*

Chapter 9
– Bringing About Change

On Belief in Players:

"A good coach will make his players see what they can be rather than what they are."
— *Ara Parseghian*

Bringing About Change

Change is inevitable. You know that. As a coach, you've come to accept and even expect change. You are ready for it. You embrace change because you understand that greater success can only come with change.

You know how to handle change ... *it's the people on your team that we are concerned about.* They are not as comfortable with change as you are. In fact, they are more likely to run from change than to embrace it.

But the fact is, change is inevitable. Your job as a coach is to help everyone on your team accept and even welcome change.

5 keys to welcoming change

How do you show those on your team that change is an opportunity to learn and grow? How can you help them actually welcome change?

You begin by giving them these five keys:

On the Basics:

"Some people try to find things in this game that don't exist, but football is only two things: blocking and tackling."

— *Vince Lombardi*

133

KEY #1 — Expect change to be good. Most fear change because they expect it to bring something bad, such as loss, failure, and pain. More often than not, change is good ... but when you are expecting it to be bad, it is.

It's really an attitude of getting what you expect. Stating that change is good is the best place to start. It needs to become a mindset. Then when unknowns and moments of pain present themselves, good things can still be expected to come as a final result.

If you will let it, change has a way of bringing about increased clarity of purpose. It defines and even refines what it is you are working toward. That can only be good!

And the fear of the unknown? When it becomes known, it's nothing to be afraid of. Change is good!

KEY #2 — Use change to grow. People want to grow personally, but the usual perception is that the team will benefit from change and they won't.

Show the team that they can use change to grow personally. Everybody can benefit from change, especially if they are looking for ways to improve.

KEY #3 — Get involved. Only those who get wet will ever learn to swim. Similarly, those who get involved in the process of handling change will be the real winners.

Change requires planning, tracking, and evaluating every new circumstance, situation, and procedure. Encourage

On Pushing Hard:

"No one has ever drowned in sweat."
— *Lou Holtz*

134

everyone to get involved. This will not only solve potential problems, but it also will empower you on a personal level.

KEY #4 — Be flexible. One of the greatest secrets to facing and handling change is flexibility (the ability to bend without breaking). When it comes to change, flexibility gives you the ability to hold on to your goals, your mission, and your cause while you do what needs to be done.

Also, flexibility makes it possible to meet the needs of the individuals while still accomplishing the organization's goals. Flexibility is good for everyone and helps everyone win.

> "Positive thinking is the key to success in business, education, pro football, anything that you can mention. I go out there thinking that I'm going to complete every pass."
> — *Ron Jaworski*

KEY #5 — Own it. Lastly, those who take ownership are the ones who will rise up to become leaders. Encourage everyone to lay claim to the changes coming their way. Grab the change and make it yours!

What's more, ownership reduces the threat of change because when they own it, they take responsibility to do what it takes to make things work.

On Earning Respect:

"Any time you give a man something he does not earn, you cheapen him. Our kids earn what they get, and that includes respect."
— *Woody Hayes*

Keep your priorities while changing

In times of constant change and challenge, it is always difficult to keep priorities straight. This is another reason why clear goals in each area of life are so valuable.

Encourage those on your team to keep their goals handy. You may know where they are going, but they might need some assistance in keeping that focus. Based on their own goals, they should be able to push aside the "cloud" that can come with change and focus on what matters most to them.

As a team, the action steps for achieving specific goals serve to determine which part of the effort will be yours and which part will be given to others on your team. I believe that the most effective way of choosing your own activities is that of determining the time cost involved for you.

Teach this important message to your team:

> Based on your annual income and the number of hours you work per week, it is possible to determine with a fair degree of accuracy what you are being paid each week, each day, and each hour on the job.
>
> When you realize what your time is really worth in terms of dollars and cents, it becomes far easier to choose the items you will perform personally and those you will delegate to others in the organization.

On Managing Change:

"You either manage change or it manages you."
— *Ron Stolski*

Comparing the cost of your time with the worth of the activity involved is an effective way to set both personal and team priorities. You should not squander a good deal of your valuable time on projects that can be handled by others for less cost.

Teaching others the value of their time is another reason why you want to train others to take your place!

Obviously, activities that help move people closer to predetermined objectives demand a higher priority than those that will produce little real benefit. Any coach's time is best spent on items that produce the highest rate of return.

> "Whatever you vividly imagine, ardently desire, sincerely believe, and enthusiastically act upon ... must inevitably come to pass!"
> — *Paul J. Meyer*

Keeping in touch with the team

Keeping in touch with your team is essential for you, for the team, and for the individual members. To maximize everyone's time, apply the following:

On Winning Now:

"No matter how much you've won, no matter how many games, no matter how many championships, no matter how many Super Bowls, you're not winning now, so you stink."
— *Bill Parcells*

#1 — Automate wherever possible. If a task or form can be automated, do so. Make as much of the "busy work" automatic as you can. That way menial projects do not take a lot of time or energy.

> "When a successful organization becomes infected with the Disease of Me, people who create 20% of the results will begin believing they deserve 80% of the rewards."
> — *Pat Riley*

Teach your team members to use the system. Every organization has a certain way of doing things. If the process works, then use it. This will help eliminate repetitive decision making and prevent accidental omission of important activities.

#2 — Update regularly. Regular updates, whether daily, weekly, or monthly, are very important. The principle is, "If you can measure it, you can manage it."

To be able to manage something, such as the pursuit of your goals, you have to know exactly where you are on the way toward accomplishing your goal.

Set up the time and the manner in which updates should occur, then stick to that schedule like glue!

On Keeping the Focus:

"I don't listen to the radio anymore. I do not read the paper anymore. Those are things that helped me, because it gave us a chance to do what we were supposed to be doing, spending time with our coaches, our players, and asking questions to people we respect."
— *Mack Brown*

#3 — Be available. You have to be available, and so do the leaders (assistants and players) you are training on your team. Being available provides direction and encouragement, which has a profound effect on the overall confidence of the team.

Let stress work for you

Change can be stressful. In fact, it usually is. The secret is to use the stress to help you in some way. Teaching your team to do the same will help them immensely.

For example, if a new play is introduced to the team, instead of emphasizing the changes it brings, focus on the increased benefits that the new play provides. By letting the stress of learning new skills push people toward better performance, the stress is seen as good rather than bad.

Over time, if stresses are not dealt with, they can do mental, physical, and emotional damage. Teach your team members to take control of stress and make it work for them. This principle is just as powerful off the field!

Since you know that change is good, the stress that comes with it cannot be all bad. Focus on the positives and use the stress to accomplish your goals faster than ever.

Change is here to stay

Change is here to stay, as long as you are pursuing your goals and reaching for even greater success. Since you

On Being the Best:

"You have to teach that youngster, you have to motivate him and help him learn to be the very best he can be."

— *Frank Kush*

and everyone on your team wants to grow and increase, accepting that change is here to stay is essential.

When you accept this truth, nothing is the same. How can you run from change when it brings profit? How can you let stress hurt you when the change it brings is really for your benefit? How can you be afraid of change when it is there to help you?

The sooner you and your team embrace change, the better. Accepting, reaching for, and even wanting change is the best guarantee of incredible growth.

That is success in the making!

On Discipline:

"I don't care what your rules and punishment are, consistency is the most important thing. We had few rules, but we stuck by the ones we had, and when you stepped over the mark, that was all she wrote. They get mad at you, but when they come back later on, they understand what you were trying to do."

— *Bill Yeoman*

On Character:

"When you have a team with character then you have a team that is going to be a winner in life, not only on the football field, but out in life after they get out of football, period."

— *Tom Landry*

Chapter 10
— *Leading Your Team*

On Increasing Your Pay:

"The more you teach, the better you are going to get paid because you are going to win more."
— *Frank Broyles*

Leading Your Team

As you take the five steps to becoming the coach you were meant to be, you will have what it takes to not only lead your team, but you also will be able to train those on your team to become leaders themselves.

Develop your team

Developing your team, either in the areas of personal growth or technical training, is vitally important. Showing that you really care about their personal goals as well as their sports goals means a great deal to them.

Most coaches (whether consciously or subconsciously) actually work to avoid training their assistants because they fear that eventually an assistant will replace them at the helm. This, however, can be a very good thing!

Look on this possibility as an incredible benefit. After all, if you don't have anyone prepared to take your place, you are destined to stay just where you are!

On Leading Others:

"Leadership is getting someone to do what they don't want to do, to achieve what they want to achieve."

— *Tom Landry*

The truth is, if you don't train others to take your place, those on your team will not train those below them either. In the end, everyone is limited because nobody wants to let go of their current position.

Let go!

Be someone who trains others to surpass you in every area, be it in personal growth or in technical know-how. Don't be afraid to train another leader to take your place. That leader will then do the same and you will have a team that is free to move forward in every area!

Lead by example

In every way, you are the role model for your team. How do you react to change? What is your belief in your potential? Do you communicate well?

Whatever the situation, *you are the example*. You are the role model, *every single day*.

This means that your attitudes establish the prevailing atmosphere of thought for your team members. Your habits of thought determine how receptive team members will be to the pursuit of excellence. Your commitment to personal and professional development determines how seriously team members approach individual and on-the-job improvement.

It's as simple as that.

On Honesty:

"If the coach isn't honest, every kid out there knows it. After all, what we're trying to do is to raise those kids out there and get them up to another level."

— *Gordon Wood*

Communicate clearly

As a coach, you must communicate clearly. This is absolutely imperative. What you say must be heard and understood. If you leave anything to chance, it will never happen.

Part of communicating clearly involves your actions ... because your actions speak louder than your words. As a result, your actions must send the right message.

> **"A great manager has a knack for making ball players think they are better than they really are."**
> — *Reggie Jackson*

For example, by keeping your word, it tells everyone on the team that you are serious, honest, and trustworthy. By doing what you do with excellence, it tells everyone that you expect nothing less. When you lead by example, you show team members what you expect them to do.

Whatever you do or say, you are communicating. Just make sure it is the message you want to send. When you leave no room for miscommunication, team members understand exactly what is going on, which is a necessary quality for successfully accomplishing goals.

Be a coach, not a critic

People want to work in an environment and be part of a team that offers them the opportunity to grow in skill and

On Confidence:

"Besides pride, loyalty, discipline, heart, and mind, confidence is the key to all the locks."
— *Joe Paterno*

responsibility. In short, they just want to be free to reach more of their unlimited potential.

As a coach, you play a part in this effort by delegating, training, and promoting people. Along the way, you will be either their coach or their critic.

Coaching is an ongoing process, not a one-time event. If people are truly serious about improving and getting better, then they need a coach who will help them do just that. Even if they are not serious, by being a coach you are still giving them a chance. In time, they will probably move on.

Either way, there is no need for criticism. It builds no loyalty, hurts the people who want to learn, and causes people to look for opportunities elsewhere.

Being a coach, on the other hand, attracts good people, brings out the best in them, and enables those on your team to reach their goals. Everyone wins!

Avoid these leadership traps

Much of coaching know-how comes from experience. That's just the way it is. In my mind, however, if you find a way to shorten the learning curve, that is a good thing!

Here are several coaching traps you can avoid, simply by understanding what they are and what they can do to hurt you:

On Losing Good Players:

"We're not in the NFL. We don't get Brett Favre for 14 years. When you lose one, you have to find somebody else and figure out what he can do best."

— *Mack Brown*

• *Doing Too Much:* The failure to delegate properly can trap you under a pile of too much paperwork, too many details to handle, and too little time for creative planning and management.

Essentially, your attitude is the culprit. When you believe in your people, train them well, and give them the opportunity to accept responsibility for significant projects, you avoid this problem altogether.

• *Doing Too Little:* The damage from not delegating enough can be just as bad as the damage from delegating too much.

If you are over-delegating, you are not doing enough research to see if the individual is adequately trained, has "bought into" the team's vision, or may simply be either over-whelmed or incompetent for the job.

Those who do not do enough research are out-of-touch coaches. They have lost control of the team and therefore, no longer have influence on the team's direction.

You can avoid this trap by keeping a written up-to-date plan for delegating, along with an implementation schedule that includes details of what is to be delegated and to whom.

• *Forgetting Your Personal Growth:* It is easy for coaches to be so focused on a goal or on leading a team that they forget to work on their own personal growth.

On Doing All You Can:

"The only thing that I would say is try to be a kind coach to your people and players. Just do everything that you can for your players."
— *Don Coryell*

Never assume that you have learned all you need to learn, have developed all the skills required for continued success, or have become all that your potential allows. The truth is, no matter what you have accomplished to date, you still have more potential for success available for immediate use.

That is why working to achieve balance in all six areas of your life is so important. You can't neglect your personal growth when you are actively working on it and have written it down as one of your goals.

• *Accepting Average Work:* Pursuing excellence is hard work. That's why many coaches make the mistake of accepting mediocrity from their team members and from themselves. But average work is not going to bring the desired success.

There is only one standard that you want: excellence. The surest way to maintain that standard is to lead by example. When you do excellent work, the expectation on everyone else is to do excellent work.

• *Failing to Notice Strengths:* Every person has talents or abilities that can benefit the team. Your job is to keep your eye out for those talents and abilities while simultaneously

On Delegating:

"The first thing that you want to do when you're given the opportunity to be a head coach is surround yourself with the best people you can find out there, and then once you get these people, give them the opportunity to do the job. Let them coach."

— *Don Shula*

teaching team members what they need to learn to accomplish the team's goals.

Most coaches don't study their people, look for their strengths, or ask about their personal goals. The infamous square-peg-in-a-round-hole debacle is the usual result. People are expected to do certain things that don't suit them, and over time this drains all the energy and creativity out of them. Eventually, they either quit or are fired.

> **"The difference between the impossible and the possible lies in a man's determination."**
> — *Tommy Lasorda*

Instead, be proactive! Look for ways to help people find what they do well. Help them with their weaknesses, and don't force them into a dead-end job. Be the type of coach you would want to have!

• *Guarding the Status Quo:* You've heard it said, "If it ain't broke, don't fix it." Though at times this is true, as a coach, you cannot maintain the status quo forever. Refusing to change to meet new demands is a sure recipe for disaster and is usually the result of not understanding the psychology of change.

When faced with change, we all begin with the *Shock and Denial* phase. We deny change at this point, claiming it is not necessary for every reason we can think of. Then

On Building a Team:

"You must learn how to hold a team together. You lift some men up ... calm others down ... until finally, they've got one heartbeat. Then, you've got yourself a team."

— *Bear Bryant*

comes the *Resistance and Anger* phase where we try to resist and fight against the inevitable. Next, if we are still moving forward, is the *Adaptation and Acceptance* phase where we begin to accept and adapt to the required change. Finally, we encounter the *Commitment and Results* phase. It is here that we become committed to the change and follow through to make it happen.

When you understand the psychology of change, and work through every phase yourself, you understand the process. You can then help those on your team work through the same phases to ensure that change is accepted.

As a coach, you must learn the balance of pushing for change while maintaining order. The status quo, on the other hand, is a trap to avoid.

• *Ignoring Problems:* The absolute best way to handle problems is to solve them before they occur. This is all part of anticipating potential roadblocks and obstacles.

The next best way to handle problems is to have clear procedures in place that treat problems as part of the normal routine as well as handle those problems.

Problems don't go away on their own. It's the people who go away. Ignoring problems is another way of telling a team member, "You are not important."

On Belief in Staff:

"I think that it's important that you have good people, and once they become your people they are good people, they are the best people. They are the best coaching staff in the country, whoever you may be working with."

— *Vince Dooley*

As a coach, if a problem does occur, handle it quickly. Do the research or bring in the right people to find a solution right away. Waiting to address problems is a deadly trap.

• *Communicating Ineffectively:* Explaining, listening, and giving feedback are incredibly powerful tools that great coaches have mastered. Those who fail to communicate effectively are killing their team. It's like taking a knife to a balloon; there will be nothing left.

You absolutely must communicate effectively, not only so your goals can be accomplished, but also so team members can learn, grow, and accomplish their goals.

> **"Keep your mind on your objective, and persist until you succeed. Study, think and plan."**
> **— W. Clement Stone**

Interestingly, there is no gray area with communication. There is no faking it. You are either effective or ineffective, and everyone knows it! Oh, to be on the team of an effective communicator!

5 signs a coach is about to be fired

The coach who, for any reason, ceases to motivate himself to higher goals is in real trouble — or is at least on the road to danger. What are the signs? Generally, there are five danger signals that warn a coach that his own motivation

On Belief in Others:

"Treat a person as he is, and he will remain as he is. Treat him as he could be, and he will become what he should be."

— *Jimmy Johnson*

is on the wane. These symptoms can manifest themselves in the following forms:

1) Doubt: Doubting yourself and your ability to do the job that you are being paid to do. Self-confidence is lost; worry and confusion take over.

2) Procrastination: — Putting off important decisions; hesitating to take considered risks; hoping the problem will take care of itself.

3) Pride: — Surrendering to pride, egotism, and status seeking; coveting the title of the job instead of concentrating on better ways and new ideas for actually doing the job; desiring to be a "well-thought-of" man instead of a thinking man.

4) Complacency: — Surrendering to the inner urge that almost everyone has to "take it easy"; being satisfied with "good enough" instead of "good," and "good" instead of "excellent."

5) Loss of Purpose: — Lacking mental provisions or concrete plans for going anywhere else; the first goal becomes the end of the career instead of another beginning.

The coach who exhibits one of more of these danger signals has lost his motivation. He is adrift, with no plan, no

On the Right Player:

"If you can't hug 'em, pat 'em, and brag about 'em, you don't want 'em on the team."

— *Lou Holtz*

purpose, and no pattern by which to live. And although he may not realize it, he faces a certain future ... being fired!

The benefits of paying the price

Developing your full potential, as a coach and as an individual, involves an incredible amount of hard work. This is as it should be, for all lasting growth comes with a price. If it were free, it would not be nearly as meaningful or beneficial.

Some goals will be accomplished quickly, while others may take years to complete. Either way, the return on your investment will make the effort worthwhile. Here are some of the benefits of becoming a great coach:

• *Money and Influence:* Great coaches *rise to the top* and invariably *make more money* and *have more influence*. That's the way it works ... and you deserve it!

• *Relationships:* Coaching is about people. After all, you lead people, not things. You lead people *through the relationships you form* with them, and as time goes by, these friendships *will be some of the most meaningful* that you will ever form with people. *You've been through a lot together and it creates a bond that can last a lifetime.*

On Correcting Your Staff:

"I never criticized a coach on the field or in public or anywhere else. Now we might get together and have a discussion. And I know full well that is the reason I've won a lot of football games."

— *Gordon Wood*

• *Respect and Trust:* By leading as you would like to be led, you gain the respect and trust of each team member, their family members, and those in the community. This will bring you even more opportunities for personal growth and service to others.

• *Goals Accomplished:* Seeing your goals achieved is in itself an incredible reward. The benefits of those goals are yours to enjoy.

• *Something to Offer:* The better coach you are, the more you have to offer. You know those on your team have benefitted and that encourages you to reach out to more people. You have something to offer and you know it! That feels good.

• *Team Spirit:* When you work closely with people to reach a common goal, you create a strong team bond. Add in the fact that you are actually helping them reach their own goals and you have an incredible team spirit. Team members become like family and you find joy in helping them achieve success.

On Giving Others Credit:

"Give them credit too. You don't want to be the one who sits there and takes all the credit. When you have assistant coaches who are doing a great job, you want to make sure that you mention them and give them credit for the good job that they do for you."

— *Don Shula*

This team spirit is so attractive that people are willing to make great sacrifices just to be part of your team. They know that what they will gain by being associated with you will easily surpass anything they have to give up. There is power in team spirit!

Likewise, the benefits of becoming a great coach make the price you pay almost insignificant!

On Selfishness:

"Nothing devastates a football team like a selfish player. It's a cancer."

— *Paul Brown*

Chapter 11
— Coach ... Who Is Going to Motivate You?

On Attitude:

"Indomitable in victory, insufferable in defeat."
— *Woody Hayes*

Coach ... Who Is Going to Motivate You?

One of the greatest challenges faced by every coach in today's super-charged sports environment is this: **How can a coach, who must continually work to motivate others, recharge his own batteries and re-motivate himself?**

The question begs for answers. How many times in your career have you seen examples like these:

- **A talented, capable, fast-rising coach is promoted — and begins a rapid slide to oblivion.**

- **A coach, after a brilliant climb up the coaching ladder, is named head coach — and finds that the fire has gone out.**

On Self-Motivation:

"You can motivate by fear, and you can motivate by reward. But both those methods are only temporary. The only lasting thing is self motivation."

— *Homer Rice*

- **The coach of a once successful team struggles to increase the team's standings, and just as he begins to reap the rewards, he hears that he might be fired.**

The secret to staying motivated

What happened? Do you still have the same drive, the determination, and the consuming ambition that seemed almost inexhaustible just a few short years ago? Do you still possess the same powerful self-motivator?

George Bernard Shaw, about a year before his death, granted a rare interview to a well-known journalist. The reporter's questions were designed to lead the famous English playwright to reminisce, and one of the best questions was: "Mr. Shaw, you have known some of the greatest men of our time — statesmen, artists, philosophers, writers, and musicians — and you've outlived most of them. Suppose it were possible for you to call back on of them. Which one would it be? What man do you miss the most?"

Without hesitation, Shaw, whose biting wit had made him internationally famous, reported, "The man I miss the most is the man I used to be!"

You don't have to be 80 years old, as Shaw was, to be able to look back at "the man I used to be." But reminiscing or looking back has little value unless you have reason for it. When you compare yourself with what you were yesterday, what differences do you find? That is useful information!

On Living Life:

"Don't go to the grave with life unused."
— *Bobby Bowden*

Do you still rise to the challenge of coaching or do you find yourself drained of inspiration by the demands of the position because others are looking to you for motivational impetus? How do you go about motivating others and at the same time motivating yourself? In short, who motivates the motivator?

The beginning is not the end

I knew a young man in the Army who anxiously awaited the day of his return to civilian life. He planned to go into business for himself; and, to implement that plan, he carefully saved every cent he could. He laid meticulous plans for every step of his venture. He was experienced in the specialized field he had chosen, and he lacked neither business acumen nor common sense. His achievement-motivation was so strong that failure seemed impossible.

> "If you can dream it, you can do it. Always remember that this whole thing was started by a mouse."
> — Walt Disney

Within six months after his separation from the Army, he had established his business. He worked without respite to protect his investment of time and money. Although the business was not large, it began to grow and showed promise of becoming a profitable enterprise. The first year, business was good; the second year, prospects were even better.

On Moving Up:

"I didn't want a guy to come in and just work. I wanted him to be motivated to become a head coach."

— *Hayden Fry*

159

However, before the end of the third year, something began to happen. Business took a turn for the worse, and if the cause was not immediately apparent, at least the results were. During the fourth year, the business reached a definite state of decline as my friend scrambled frantically to plug the sinking ship.

The straw that broke the camel's back came in the form of a vigorous, hard-hitting competitor. My friend's business went under. All his dreams ended in a neat blue folder that contained his pleadings of bankruptcy. Today he works for the man who, he still believes, "put him out of business."

Although my friend is still asking himself "Why?" the answer isn't too hard to find: **he mistook the beginning of achievement for the end!**

In two short years, he had become an acknowledged success, not only by business-rating standards, but, more important, in his own estimation. It was here that he made the mistake of his life: he concluded that the goal he had been working toward was already an accomplished fact. His self-motivation was gone. He no longer worked as hard as he had during those first two years — not because of laziness, but because he lacked the drive toward a goal. He no longer made the careful plans in the little, but highly important, areas that had once brought him to the threshold of success. The spark

On Coaching:

"You've got to have great athletes to win, I don't care who the coach is. You cannot win without good athletes, but you can lose with them. This is where coaching can make a difference."

— Lou Holtz

was gone, and he allowed his enthusiasm to cool before he got "inside" and had the door closed firmly behind him.

I'm sure all coaches know others who have made the same mistake. They spend years working day and night to achieve a planned goal, but once there, all the drive that brought them to their coveted position melts away. They run out of steam. As they gaze at their wall of trophies and jerseys and game balls ... their dream world slips from under them.

Here is reality: *If a coach does this, how much more does a player do this?* As a coach, it is your responsibility to be self-motivated and to teach your players to be self-motivated. Success is not permanent and a goal accomplished is never the end of the road.

The truth is that once you reach a goal, you must work twice as hard as before. You must continue to be creative or you must be content to wither. When your enthusiasm atrophies, the whole team dries up, too. Your successor is at the door! You must maintain the very qualities of drive and initiative that got you to your position in the first place.

> "Even if you are on the right track, you'll get run over if you just sit there."
> — **Will Rodgers**

The late Fritz Kreisler applied this principle in his own professional life. As is common with most concert violinists, Kreisler maintained a rigorous eight-hour daily practice

On Teamwork:

"When a team outgrows individual performance and learns team confidence, excellence becomes a reality."

— *Joe Paterno*

schedule throughout his entire career. Asked why he continued such practice after he had become world-famous for musical excellence, he explained, "If I neglect to practice for a month, my audience knows the difference. If I neglect it for a week, my wife knows the difference. If I neglect practice for a day, Fritz Kreisler can tell the difference!" No amount of fame and fortune could lull Kreisler into a false sense of security, and away from the standard he had set for himself.

Self-motivation has no time-outs

Sometimes, the fruits of our early labors — the title, the office, the praise, the authority, and the prestige — lull us into the false illusion that we no longer need to push and motivate ourselves. We lay aside the real tools of our achievement: our minds, our hands, and our feet. We lose momentum, humility, and the human touch. Perhaps the most important missing link between our present self and the man we used to be is the lack of having someone above us to supply inspiration and motivation. For the first time, we stand alone. But this is no oversight. We are expected to stand alone. We should not have achieved executive stature unless, somewhere along the line, we had exhibited an ability to stand alone.

This brings us back to our basic question: Who motivates the motivator? Who provides the drive for the coach to whom others look for inspiration and leadership? The answer

On the Road to Success:

"The road to Easy Street goes through the sewer."

— *John Madden*

is obvious: He must motivate HIMSELF! He can no longer look to the upper echelon for "outside" inspiration. He is that "upper echelon." Once he realizes that the motivation for his continued success must come from himself, he can proceed with the proper steps to achieve it. He can build a comprehensive program of personal motivation that will keep him moving steadily forward. He can and he must "press on." He cannot stand still.

Everyone who wants counsel or help in building a program of personal motivation can find it. Personally, I've always been an avid reader of motivational books, inspirational stories, and biographies of successful men in all walks of life. It isn't that I have a great deal of spare time; rather, I have found the experience so rewarding that I make time for it.

> **"It's what you learn after you know it all that counts."**
> — *John Wooden*

I find that this vicarious association with successful men helps to fill me with the same drive and determination that made them successful. I've learned from men whom I've never met that the only real limitations I shall ever encounter are those that I place on myself.

How to motivate the motivator!

How do you motivate the motivator? What's the secret? You know the secret. You've read it already. Here it is again: ***The way to stay motivated is to set goals and then***

On Jumping In:

"The man who tried his best and failed is superior to the man who never tried."
— *Bud Wilkinson*

pursue those goals. Step by step, here is the success formula that will get you where you want to go:

#1 — Crystallize your thinking. Set a definite goal for yourself with a definite time limit for its achievement. Nebulous generalities, such as "wealthy by middle-age" will not suffice. Set a goal of earning an exact amount, to the last penny, by a certain date. You must know exactly where you want to go before you can ever hope to arrive.

#2 — You must have a plan for the attainment of your goal. You'll be surprised at how quickly a plan will change you from a wandering generality into a meaningful specific. Write down your concrete plan. Put it into outline form with intermediate steps that can be checked off frequently to show signs of progress; but NEVER check off a step as completed until work has already begun on the next step. This is insurance against stopping short of the goal.

#3 — You must develop a burning desire to reach your goal through the use of your plan. Make an exhaustive list of all possible benefits of reaching your goal. Include all the improvements to yourself, your financial condition, your personality, and your abilities. List the ways in which achieving your goal will benefit your family, your team, and even the community. Write down this list and keep it with you, adding to it as you discover new advantages; subtracting only as your values change (and they will).

On Giving Your Best:

"Nobody who ever gave his best regretted it."
— *George Halas*

As you recognize the benefits to be gained, you are automatically accumulating desire. As the desire becomes stronger, your personality will take on a dynamic magnetism that draws everything to you and makes your goal possible.

#4 — You must also maintain unshakable faith in yourself and in your ability to accomplish your purpose. Put modesty aside and list every positive attribute and ability you have. Make the list long as is truthful. Then, make a study of one man or of several men who have already achieved success. Note particularly the qualities and compare them with yours. You will be amazed at the similarity!

> **"Great works are performed not by strength, but by perseverance."**
> — *Samuel Johnson*

You will find that you already possess the tools, so have confidence in them and use them.

#5 — You must create a force of iron-willed determination that will blast any obstacle from your path. If the benefits of achieving your goal are worthwhile, any person or situation that gets in the way is a thief, stealing your future success. Remember that any obstacle conceived by the mind of man can be overcome by the mind of another man filled with desire and determination. Make your determination so

On Keeping the Door Open:

"Do not close your door or your heart to your players. As leaders, we are obligated to do the right thing."

— **Ron Stolski**

strong that it will eliminate any situation or circumstance that stands in the way of your goal.

Dr. Roger Bannister, the first person to run a 4-minute mile, is a great example of someone who applied these five steps to reaching a goal.

He crystallized his thinking — to run a mile in less than four minutes.

He developed a plan to do it — he set out to run the first three-quarters of the mile in less than three minutes. (He knew that if he could accomplish that much, he would automatically run the last quarter in less than one minute.)

He developed a burning desire — he practiced constantly, with his specific goal in mind.

He believed strongly that he could do it — he said the feat was more a result of mental attitude than of physical conditioning and training. (He explained that he knew he needed to first make up his mind and convince himself that he could break the record before his mind would allow his body to do it.)

He created an iron-willed determination that would not be denied — and he did it. Once he had developed his plan and the detailed procedures to accomplish his goal, he carried out his plan, breaking the 4-minute mile barrier!

An interesting reaction soon followed. Others began breaking the 4-minute mile with relative ease! The point?

On Improvement:

"There's nothing that cleanses your soul like getting the hell kicked out of you."
— *Woody Hayes*

Physical ability is secondary to the mental conditioning that is necessary to meet a goal!

Whatever your goal, when you have taken these five steps, you are on your way to reach your goals! You are also self-motivated! And that is how you motivate the motivator.

On Being a Role Model:

"Don't ever walk by a child without stopping and shaking his hand or signing an autograph because that is what we are supposed to do. That's the role model we are supposed to be."

— *Mack Brown*

Chapter 12
— *Conclusion*

Conclusion

It comes down to choice. *You have chosen to become the coach you were meant to be.* Congratulations!

Many on your team, whether assistants or players, are also making the choice of whether they will become leaders or not. They must step up to the plate, as you have, and make the decision to become the coach, the player, and the leader they were meant to be!

You cannot force them. It is a personal choice. They have to want it like you did. When they do make that decision, be there for them. Encourage them. Help them. Train them.

In time, the next generation of leaders will step forward and new leaders will do what you've done.

That is when you'll know that you've become the coach you were meant to be!

On Your Destiny:

"You are the keeper of the greatest game we teach, football."

— *Ron Stolski*

Your Notes & New Ideas

Your Notes & New Ideas

Personal Leadership Questions

These questions are indicators of your progress in your personal efforts to become the coach you were meant to be:

QUESTION #1: Have I crystallized my thinking so that I know where I stand now and where I want to go?

QUESTION #2: Are my vision, mission, and purpose statements clear to me and to my team members?

QUESTION #3: Do I have a detailed, written plan to achieve each important personal and organizational goal, and have I set a deadline for their attainment?

QUESTION #4: Are my personal goals balanced with the need to help my organization achieve?

QUESTION #5: Do my personal goals represent a balance among the six areas of life?

QUESTION #6: Do I have a burning desire to achieve the goals I have set for myself?

QUESTION #7: Have I developed within my team members and myself a passion for achieving the success we've envisioned?

QUESTION #8: Do I have supreme confidence in my ability to reach these goals?

QUESTION #9: Do I trust my team members to strive toward success and to continue to develop more of their innate potential for achievement?

QUESTION #10: Have I accepted personal responsibility for the success of my team — and for the achievement of my own personal goals?

QUESTION #11: Do I possess the iron-willed determination to follow through regardless of circumstances or what others say, think, or do?

Your Goals in All Six Areas of Life

The key to Becoming a Total Person is to set and achieve meaningful goals in all six areas of life. Below, jot down several ideas for goals in each area — goals that are personally meaningful to you and that will motivate you to use more of your full potential.

Goals for the Family/Home Area:

- _____
- _____
- _____
- _____
- _____
- _____

Goals for the Financial/Career Area:

- _____
- _____
- _____
- _____

- _____

- _____

Goals for the Mental/Educational Area:

- _____

- _____

- _____

- _____

- _____

Goals for the Physical/Health Area:

- _____

- _____

- _____

- _____

- _____

- _____

Goals for the Social/Cultural Area:

- _____

- _____

- _____

- _____

- _____

- _____

Goals for the Spiritual/Ethical Area:

- _____

- _____

- _____

- _____

- _____

- _____

Paul J. Meyer on Taking Risks

I have lived a lifetime thinking, planning, and then jumping in — of taking chances — and it has paid off handsomely for me.

People ask about different businesses I have started and how I knew when I had enough information to jump in. I tell them I always ask myself these questions:

- **What are my goals?**

- **Can I reach my goal without taking a risk?**

- **What are the benefits if I take this chance?**

- **What can I lose by taking a chance — by risking?**

- **What can I do to prevent these losses?**

- **Is the potential loss I am thinking about greater than the possible gain?**

- **Is this the right time to take this action?**

- **What pressures are on me to make this decision?**

- **What would I have to know to change my mind about taking this risk?**

- **How much experience do I have with this type of risk?**

- Who is someone I can confide in or ask for advice about this risk?

- Do I have personal blind spots in my vision about this risk?

- If I take this chance — this risk — will people think more or less of me if I succeed? Do I really care?

- If a loss does occur, will I take it personally, or am I able to be realistic and objective?

- Will I worry and worry about the risk I have taken?

- Who else has made a similar investment?

- What actions can I take to track my investment and protect it?

- How will this risk affect me, my spouse, my children, my parents, my friends, my team, and my relationship with my bank?

- Do I really enjoy the lifestyle of an entrepreneur?

Fortunately, anything that has ever happened to me in my role as a leader, salesperson, business person, or investor has never affected who I am as a person or reduced my self-image. I make conscious decisions to manage my life to maintain a healthy self-image, peace of mind, and happiness.

About the Author

Paul J. Meyer learned to be a winner early in life. He:

- won first place in a national sales competition selling magazines at age 12,
- set a record picking prunes at age 16,
- set military physical fitness records at age 18,
- was the national leader of two different life insurance companies by age 22,
- built one of the largest insurance companies by single-handedly recruiting more than 800 sales associates in one year, by age 24,
- started Success Motivation Institute in 1960,
- is considered by many to be the founder of the personal development industry — sales of his programs and courses are approaching two billion dollars, more than any author in this field,
- and is also the founder of Leadership Management, Inc., Success Motivation International, Inc., Leadership Management International, Inc., plus 40 other companies involved in legal insurance, graphics/printing, computer software, real estate development, finance, publishing, manufacturing, and more.

In semi retirement, after age 70, he became a New York Times best-selling author. Some of his books include: *I Inherited a Fortune, Chicken Soup for the Golden Soul, 24 Keys That Bring Complete Success, Unlocking Your Legacy,* and *Forgiveness ... the Ultimate Miracle.* Also, he is co-authoring a book with Ken Blanchard, entitled: *Repetition, Repetition.*

Amazingly, his five children all have similar success stories as winners. One son won the decathlon in central Texas after age 35. Another son won gold, silver, and bronze medals in the Senior Olympics after age 50. Another son set many of the world's speed records as a racecar driver. His two daughters and their husbands are successful business owners — one runs a huge legal insurance marketing branch and another runs a worldwide leadership development company.

Paul is using his golden years to cascade this attitude and motivation down to his grandchildren. One of the most important things about Paul J. Meyer and his family is that they are givers. The basketball arena at Baylor is the Paul J. Meyer Arena, he has endowed chairs, built chapels, and, in a word, spent a lot of money investing in the lives of young people. It's a family affair that involves the whole family.

His grandchildren are successes as well. One is a pro golfer, another is launching his own business, and much more. With 15 grandchildren, there will be much success to report.

Paul and his wife, Jane, live in Waco, Texas.

Your Notes & New Ideas

Your Notes & New Ideas

Your Notes & New Ideas

Your Notes & New Ideas

Your Notes & New Ideas

Your Notes & New Ideas

Your Notes & New Ideas

Your Notes & New Ideas

Your Notes & New Ideas